Elphame

A Journey into Elven Light

Alan Richardson

'Alan Richardson has been writing weird, winsome and frequently embarrassing books for longer than many of his readers have been alive and is insanely proud of that fact. He has done biographies of such luminaries as Dion Fortune, Aleister Crowley, Christine Hartley, William G. Gray and his own grandfather George M. Richardson M.M. & Bar. Plus novels and novellas that are all set in his local area, along with scripts of same. He has a deep interest in Earth Mysteries, Mythology, Paganism, Celtic lore, Ancient Egypt, jet fighters, army tanks 1917-16, Wiltshire tea shops, Great British Actors and Newcastle United Football Club. He does not belong to any group or society and does not take pupils because most of the time he hasn't a clue what is going on.'

I don't have a web site, agent or manager, am not on LinkedIn, don't do blogs and am not quite as crabby as my writings might suggest. A more detailed list of my published work can be found somewhere on Amazon Books.

As before, I price this at the minimum suggested by KDP, which means that **a)** I get two pence for every copy I sell. **b**) hopefully people might be tempted to buy one.

Anyone with a pressing need to contact me can do so via: *alric@blueyonder.co.uk* but please don't attach your manuscripts and ask for 'an honest opinion', because I don't want to hurt people, and will always fib.

Dedicated to…

Our grandchildren while they are still at the Elfin stages of their wondrous lives: Cassidy, Kara, Reuben, Jacob, Saffi, Erin, Harry and Marley.

Una Woodruff, faery *inspiratrice* at the source of the River Biss.

Basil Thomas for his puckish enchantments and always having the last Word.

Margaret, A childe of Earth whose race is of the starry heavens

Some **published books**

Geordie's War – foreword by Sting
Aleister Crowley and Dion Fortune
The Inner Guide to Egypt *with Billie John*
Priestess - the Life and Magic of Dion Fortune (but only read the updated and expanded and revised Thoth Publications version and not the previous editions)
Magical Gateways
The Magical Kabbalah
The Google Tantra - How I became the first Geordie to raise the Kundalini. *new edition retitled as*…Sex and Light – How to Google your way to God Hood.
The Old Sod *with* Marcus Claridge
Working with Inner Light *with Jo Clark*
Earth God Rising
Earth God Risen
Gate of Moon
Dancers to the Gods
Inner Celtia *with David Annwn*
Letters of Light
Me, mySelf and Dion Fortune
Bad Love Days
Short Circuits
The Templar Door
Searching for Sulis
The Quantum Simpleton
The Sea Priest
Dark Magery
Al-Khemy
Visions at Ewyas
Visions of Paviland
Neurolithica – foreword by Uri Geller
Kim's Book
The Inner Realms of Christine Hartley
Scattering Light – with (somehow) the shade of *William G. Gray*

Fiction
The Giftie
On Winsley Hill
The Fat Git – the Story of a Merlin
The Great Witch Mum – *illustrated by Caroline Jarosz*
Dark Light – a neo-Templar Time Storm
The Movie Star
Shimmying Hips
du Lac
The Lightbearer

Twisted Light
The Moonchild
The Giftie – in her own words.
Old Light
Boudicca – scripted with Mark Colmar

As Yet Unpublished and un-filmed Scripts

On Winsley Hill
The Enchanter (from the novella The Fat Git)
The Giftie

Introduction

As an Ancient Brit, and a proud one in terms of both age and identity, I should apologise for the use of a very American term to describe the following book…. Elphame 101.

The whole concept of Elphame came to me quite unexpectedly, as I will soon explain. Right from the start, I decided that I would try – somehow - to enter Elphame in my own way and explain what I was doing without recourse to the many very learned books and on-line discourses from recognised authorities. More importantly (at least for me), I would try to do this from within my own very limited geographical locale, and one with no obvious underlying mythological strata.

As an Ancient Brit still recovering from a major heart attack, I will no longer be able to make actual pilgrimages to Elphame-ish portals such as the Eildon Hills in the Scottish Borders or the Hen Hole in Northumberland, or the The Hill of Uisneach in Ireland, or even into the wonderful folds of the Welsh Marches that aren't too far from where I live now. Nor do I have the enviable psychism that enables visionaries I know and respect to enter at will the faery realms that so fascinate me.

Yet I've always felt somewhat empowered by that card from the Smith/Waite tarot pack known as the The Chariot.

The vehicle is actually a cubic block of solid stone, in which the man (or is it actually a woman?) is sealed. But the winged powers of Light and Darkness are at his command. Without moving anywhere, he travels everywhere. He might seem physically constrained but he is surrounded by stars He just needs a bit of armour to stop himself getting bashed about on his inwards journeys that explore the Cosmos.

There is also a quote by Lao Tzu, from chapter 47 of the *Tao Te Ching* that I've always felt summed up this card (and me) exactly, and makes everyone reading this now to be 'the sage' in question:

Without going outside, you may know the whole world.
Without looking through the window, you may see the ways of heaven.
The farther you go, the less you know.
Thus the sage knows without travelling;
He sees without looking;
He works without doing.

I haven't used Chapters with their headings. I've just wanted the whole thing to flow, as life flows.

I could say a lot more, but might feel I was getting trapped in a narrative that is alien to the spirit of Elphame itself. I do believe that whether you live in the heart of an American megalopolis, a British industrial conurbation and/or feel yourself to be as psychic as a brick, that it is still possible in non-intellectual, non-academic ways to get your own hints of the shimmering boundaries of your own private Elphame...

In *your* Beginnings...

Sometimes, significant things happen without people realising they *are* significant. They don't burst into your awareness like some thick envelope filled with cash being squeezed through your letterbox that sets your mind racing, heart pounding and knees trembling. Not that that's an everyday occurrence *chez* Richardson, but you get what I mean. The significant event in this case was a dream that came to me on the morning of April 30th. Apparently, all sorts of things were going on in the heavens at that period, as people were complaining on-line about Mercury being retrograde; as I'm not an astrologer that didn't mean anything. In fact it wasn't much of a 'dream' at all. Think instead of all the old movies you've seen where events in the world were described by screaming newspaper headlines: *Titanic Sinks! King Abdicates! War Ends!* Mine was like that.

The dream itself flashed into me at exactly 8.00, because I came awake then after a long night's sleep. I remember the sun coming into the window and a chattering of sparrows in our eaves and a clattering of the plastic blue bins from the (always early) Refuse Lorry outside... and then two brief images sprang into my mind.

Well, I'm still calling it a 'dream', but that implies a story-line of unlikely characters and events. This was just a simple picture. Of a newspaper. There was no-one holding it.

First one side, then the other was shown me. It had a yellowy parchment quality and there was only one word on it, yet printed innumerable times with, I seemed to see, slight variations of size and spelling: *Elphame.*

The second side seemed to be an appeal for a lost person from a particular place of that name. You know the sort of thing in the personal columns of tabloids: *Jack Black last seen 30 years ago in Whitehaven. If anyone knows his whereabouts...*

I can still see the image writ large before my brow, three days later: The first side was plastered with the Name; the second side (that I seemed to be able to read simultaneously) was also concerned with the notion of Place.

I can't pretend the name was completely unknown. I'd clearly heard of it before but couldn't have summoned up any mythic or spiritual details. *Something to do with... Something to do with...*

In the Olden Days before the Flood (of social media and the Internet) I would have scurried to find my battered copy of the *The White Goddess* by Robert Graves as the first and then only resource. In fact I've just done exactly that but my old copy is neither in our Upper Room where we keep the best and most esoteric books, nor in any of the more exoteric shelves of our house. As I have regular bursts of giving books away to local charity shops, I must have culled it years ago.

On the other hand, having just looked at the same shelf for the third time, there it is, between Zecharia Sitchin's *The 12ᵗʰ Planet* and Jim Schnabel's *Remote Viewing.* I'd like to make a story about it having disappeared into another dimension until I was ready for it, but I'm sure that the old phrase: *I couldn't see for looking* is more appropriate for the old man I am now. I'll keep an eye on it though, just in case. Our house does seem to have some sort of benign (so far) 'trog' (for lack of a better name) that can make things disappear.

None of this is familiar to me. Of course it must have flickered at the edges of my mind in previous decades. I'm reminded of those animations I used to make for my children, that I'm sure many of you would have done too: a blank note book, a little stick figure drawn on the bottom right corner, altered slightly on each page, so that when the pages are flicked through the drawing – usually of me getting bashed with a frying pan – came alive.

So, what do the flickering pages of Graves tell me via the White Goddess? Well, not a lot. At least not a lot that I feel an immediate urge to explore. In fact I was rather dismayed by the index which gave me: *Elphame, Elfin, Elfland, or Faerie.* I honestly never thought about the last three when the newspaper flapped in front of my awareness. Elfin, of course! Elfland. Faerie. No doubt Thomas the Rhymer from Erceldoun will get a Gravesian mention in the bulk of the sometimes unfathomable text. But I don't want that lot. These days everyone into Otherness either climbs onto the electric bandwagon marked 'Quantum' that goes in opposite ways at the same time, or else hitches onto the charming 'Elfin' one made of wood and wands and flowers and ferns and trundles through the eternal Wildwood.

The newspaper told me quite certainly, again and again via a thousand blurry but certain words: El*phame*. This had to be slightly different, and relevant to me personally, otherwise, why come into my psyche? And how might it be purely relevant to anyone reading this?

I must have a ponder.

It's the Coronation tomorrow, and I'm not sure whether I should attend via the telly, or go walking amid the ocean of bluebells in Friary Woods, where we always get an almost sensory feeling for the 'elfin', if I can call it that, amid the Carthusian echoes from the nearby friary itself. Something emanates from the bluebells: a feeling of purity, all's well with the worlds, Spring is a-coming, look but don't touch, breathe, peace peace peace…

I wasn't going to watch the Coronation but I did. The bluebells will always come again quickly. What I have to say next makes no sense, but I'm reminded, out of the corner of my mind, of a telly programme from the 60s. American. About lawyers: *The Defenders*. Every episode began with the words: *Democracy is a very poor form of government, but all the others are so much worse*. Aged 9, I had no idea what democracy was, but the tone and rhythm of the words stayed in my mind. I don't know much more about democracy now, aged 72, but as I saw the rituals and ceremonies of the Coronation enfolding on our small telly the boy inside helped me modify this to: *Constitutional Monarchy is a very poor form of government, but all the others are so much worse*.

I'd already noted the prominent Green Man on all the Royal invitations. There is, it seems, a secret tradition that while the farmers of the House of Saxe-Coburg-Gotha (aka the House of Windsor) might have a tedious and highly-disputed bloodline post-Richard III, all was made magickally well by the purer Spenser bloodline of Diana. And that their first born, William, was the destined Once and Future King who would balance all manner of things. As for Harry, he seems to have taken on the role of 'tanist', the Dark Twin described by Robert Graves in *The White Goddess*, whose destiny is to succeed or else destroy.

God Save the King! they all said, and I shed a ridiculous tear for this ridiculous institution in this ridiculously doomed Age we live in. And yes, all right, I'll now take the bullet for Charley too.

The older I get, I sometimes feel that the flows of time lie on top of each other, like rock strata. Sometimes you can poke upward through the crust and pull things down and around you; other times you can find yourself digging below, or even falling through. That's not a perfect analogy – in fact it's not even very good - but it will do for now. I've no doubt that tomorrow it will seem as though the same flows are felt as spirals, or even whirlpools with vortices. Or maybe I'll use the image of the Mummy, being endlessly enwrapped in memories, with various talismans and amulets enfolded between those swathes that define me.

I would argue, gently, that we all experience this without realising. We find ourselves reflecting on strata of experience that might have been or should have been; we summon up memories of things we have read and been influenced by, and thus have the long-dead authors right next to us, shimmering in our thoughts. Do the real and imaginary share the same world?

Hello Violet, I say, as an old but eternally youthful friend plonks herself next to me. *I think you should form a group, and call it The Inner Light.*

In your dreams, Alan...

Bear with me for a moment while I poke through a couple of thin

layers of time and briefly revisit that ridiculous piece from *The Defenders*. The programme starred E.G. Marshall. I doubt if many will remember him now, but he always stuck in my mind. I next saw him in *Superman II*, playing the US President and wearing a dreadful wig. *I won't let you down again Mr. President* said the Superman, restoring the American flag that had been uprooted by the monstrous General Zod (wonderfully hammed up by the uncanny Terence Stamp with his demand *Kneel before Zod!*). All of these characters are in my mind now, each one flowing in differing directions as they acted in differing things at differing times of my life, but all part of the peripheral light that shimmers at the edges of my mind, out of the corners of my memory. I've just ordered Terence

Stamp's *Reflections* from the library. They only charge £1.00 so it's well worth it. I'm sure it will trigger things in my search for Elphame.

As I sit here in the shiny Atrium of that library staring into space, I feel that I could probably connect *everything* in my life from that single muse on a single screen-shot. Is this what they mean by 'string theory'? I don't need to know. It could have been any number of other moments, not all of them connected with fillums, as they still call them up in Northumberland. But I'll wager that whoever reads this has just had a fleeting, trivial memory of their own, and are now seeing it bounce back and forth like reflecting images.

Actually, while I think on, get two small mirrors and hold them at either side of your head. If you angle your vision and the glass you will see yourself reflecting away to infinity. All of those heads you glimpse are alternative lives. Mirrors, it seems, are doorways into Elphame. The mirror-image of the what you see is part of the Mystery. Which is why meres or lakes or deep, still ponds are often access points. Elphame, I feel, can only be seen in a special state of being

Plus I'm old enough now to know how these things work out. The law of the 'Seven Degrees of Separation' is a pleasant exercise that everyone indulges in at some time. I'm sure anyone reading this will be able to connect with me personally, somehow, very quickly and lightly. And no doubt someone will whisper and tell me that E.G. Marshall was a 33° Freemason and founder of the Skull and Bones society or something equally unlikely. And the more whimsically I muse, I tell myself that, actually, if I'll now take the bullet for Charley, I'd certainly in the past have knelt before Zod. I should get out more.

You get the idea. I cannot say too often that there was NOTHING mystical about Mr. Marshall in the bad wig, or anything profound or meaningful to me about the voice-over concerning Democracy. That simply flapped into my mind like a pigeon loose within Westminster Abbey and probably crapping all over the Gentry and the Good People.

Before I get onto the topic of watches, witches and wazzocks, I should mention a simple magickal technique I devised very many years ago that you can try now. In fact do it with this book, or some small item next to you.

I tried this first with, I think, a small toy that came from a cheap Xmas Cracker. This was nothing to do with psychometry. It was a small plastic soldier. I just held it in my hand and felt the texture, and looked at the lines, then imagined who first designed this. Where were they? Did they draw it first? How did they get it made? Who designed the mould? Where? What did they think when the first one appeared? Did they show it to their family? So for a brief moment in Wiltshire on Christmas Day a teeny part of my consciousness was in Hong Kong where this was probably designed and made. What if I actually tracked this down and turned up on someone's doorstep? Would this be an arrestable offence?

It was not a matter of asking intellectual questions, but allowing the mind to flow.

I later used (and use) this at ancient sites: How was *this* small stone chosen? Where from? Why this particular place on the long barrow? Who helped? What were they feeling? What was the weather like?

Or at a medieval site… Who designed the iron knocker of this church door? What was in his or her mind to create this design? Did it come straight from the forge? What did they feel when they bashed on the door with it? Does the iron contains memories?

You get the idea. You can do it with modern artefacts too, of course, but they lack a certain ambience.

But always try to remember – to feel – that the one thing you will have in common with Lost Time and forgotten souls is that you have known love. As they would have known love. Yes, yes it sounds mawkish, wet and wussy, but it's the opener of ways that I hope will take me into Elphame.

I'll come back to that later, if I don't swirl away. I decided that when the 'Elphame Herald' tabloid appeared before my radiant brow I really didn't want spend my hours diving into arcane books like the *White Goddess* and following the myths and legends. I feared that if I invoked the Google Hierophant with a few taps of my index finger on my mystick mouse, I might find myself plummeting into a very deep and musty rabbit-hole. As it was, I did catch a few lines from Wikipedia (to which I donate a princely £5.00 every year) and caught a glimpse of…

Elphame, Queen of Elphame, Northern England and Scotland, Borders, Mother Nicneven (who she!?). Plus lots of murky stuff swirling around about Salmonds and Sturgeons – big fish whose scales everyone should try to avoid touching.

How does this relate to me? I needed to know. The 'hame' from Elphame, according to the wicked wiki, was Scottish of course. And as a Northumbrian born and bred (though now exiled) I was not unfamiliar with the Border Country and what lay beyond. In fact borders of any kind, even those artificial ones between the counties and countries, always excite me. Does that sound sad? I suppose it does. But they are – or can become – liminal places. Even the gate between one part of our long garden into the next, where the shed is, can become an entrance to faery. You don't have to see it in any psychic sense, or join any wiccan coven; you just have to acknowledge that it's there.

I'd forgotten about the watches, witches and wazzocks hadn't I?

Well, at about the same time the *Elphame Herald* flapped into my consciousness I'd had a light dream about wearing three very different watches on the same wrist. No more to it than that. I asked Margaret what that might mean and she felt it was me being in differing time streams. That's rather a nice idea, and I'd like to use it. Then I woke one morning with my solitary *actual* watch lying beside me on the pillow. I never take my watch off at night – or indeed at any time except to shower – and the strap can only be undone with deliberate actions. It could not have slipped off. And there was no reason for me, in the night, to remove it.

Was the timeless realm of Elphame doing things? I said earlier, I think, that our house seems to have a sort of 'trog' who is not above such trickery, but he/she/it has never appeared upstairs.

That's a trivial thing in the telling, as might be said of all my attempts to enter Elphame, but it made me think about the timeless and timely things that become more important, or revealing, as I get from being merely 'old' at present, and stroll down the road to becoming 'very old'.

Oh and I mentioned the word 'wazzock', which in context might make you think it's some inner-world being alongside trolls, goblins and gnomes. Well, it might be, but I simply used it for the alliteration. As far as I know it was just an old Northumbrian word for a hopeless, irritating and generally useless person. I only ever heard it used once by a very elderly man in an old people's home. That's what he described me as, actually, because I'd bought him the wrong cigarettes from the local shop: Capstan Full Strength instead of his favourite Wild Woodbines:

Cough cough cough… Ye little wazzock!

As I sit in a cafe musing about this, I find myself time-travelling to that particular encounter. I whizz from the south-west of England in a laser-straight line to the north-east, inhabiting my 17 year-old body again with its famously spotty back and bum-fluff moustache. I'm in a place called 'Pity Me', which was – I think - a small convalescent hospital in the south of Ashington, for elderly miners. At least, that's as best as I can recall. No-one else seems to remember it. Did it really exist? I definitely took letters there when I did the Xmas Post and had tea and biscuits left for me in the small kitchen.

Maybe the stunted little man who called me a wazzock had been the avatar of a troll? It has always been said that the faery folk can shape-shift. Maybe his 'wazzock' was *not* his generation's equivalent of numpty, dork, prat, wuss, pillock (all of which I've also been called) but a specific innerworld status?

Nice try Alan, but you're stretching it a bit.

Violet...you're a long way from home. 'Pity Me' is always the end of someone's road. Go, in the name of Zod!

In truth, I only added 'wazzock' for the alliteration, so I could then glide in with the theme of 'witch', whom I must summon now...

So…

We all have a 'witch' within us. I know because my Mam told me, and it was never *ever* wise to argue with a Woman of Power, as all Geordie Women have been since the Ancient of Days, are now and always will be, worlds without end. And my (part-Scottish) Mam knew this because the Geordie dialect and that of the Borders had a phrase she used when startled by someone:

14

Ye varnigh gliffed the witch oot of iz!
Translated in these days as:
You very nearly frightened the witch out of me.

I like the thought of that. Having a witch inside me. Had this come from a long-standing folk-belief?

When I first moved permanently down to the South-west I used to blame the Vikings for the Northumbrian dialect known as Geordie. I felt sure they must have forced their lexis and syntax on us in between the raping and pillaging. We would say, for example:

Am gan yem the morn morn.

Which to us was clear as day and meant:

I'm going home tomorrow morning.

Pure Norwegian, I would tell folks here in the south-west of England when I became hostage to the Southern Softies, and took on all the aspects of Stockholm Syndrome.

But it now seems that the Danes got here first, centuries before the first Viking longboat ever sneaked up on the monks of Lindisfarne. So many contemporary Geordie words, such as *gan* ('go' – modern German *gehen*) and *bairn* ('child' - modern Danish *barn*) can still trace their roots right back to those Angles. I suppose it must be meaningful that many of our friends are Danish. When they visit, I always take them just down the road to Edington where in 878, on 12th May, we finally defeated the Great Danish Army and started to become 'England'. And today, coincidentally, is the 12th May.

One day I'll get my DNA Ancestry done to see if I can pierce the veils of Time in a different way.

So… if my Ancestors had faery lore buried deep within their psyches from the centuries before Christianity, and if subtle knowings and urges can be passed down through the generations, then maybe Mam's perception of the inner 'witch' will turn out to have first stirred its cauldrons in the bitter seas between North-east England and Denmark?

It intrigues me these days when people in my lifetime whispered about witches as though they are a separate species, different in kind rather than degree They never thought of them as ordinary people living ordinary lives within their own beliefs. No-one ever whispered such things about the local Methodists.

Much later on in my life I became exiled from Geordieland and found myself living in Wiltshire on Winsley Hill. When I lived there, people muttered about 'witches in the woods' down in the valley at Murhill, never knowing of my own 'Other' self, or the fact that I'd known the Founding Mothers of modern witchcraft, and how much they were inventing as they went along.

Paddy Slade confessed to me that she made it all up about being a 'Hereditary' Witch, but I noticed that over the years she seemed to improve her yarns depending on who was listening. All power to her broom, cauldron and athame, delightful woman that she was. There may well be a real 'Hereditary' thing now, following the three or four generations since the 1950's when Gardner and Valiente and Cochrane and Sanders and Crowther and a host of others started their crafty parthenogenesis. Although I don't think any of that lot had children to pass on their 'Witch' DNA.

Maybe it's better to think that Mam was right, that we *all* have a 'witch' within us that can be lifted to startled awareness. And if we can do that, we might find our way toward Elphame.

I felt a bit 'stuck' this morning. Felt that I might have to abandon this sequence of thoughts and leave it as an essay for someone, somewhere, or bury it forever in my PC for some electronic wizardly archaeologist to dig it out from the dust of my Valley of Kings hard-drive.

Then I had a pause on my daily walk, as I crossed the River Biss and mused for a moment on borders, edges, meres, lakes, rivers - and bridges. All of which are liminal places, if you need them to be.

There are several bridges on my daily walks that take me over this river. These are all within the limit of this old (but not ancient) town with its somewhat neglected air - as many towns have in these Post-Covid days. When the Wool Trade was at its height in centuries past, the raw power of the Biss pouring down from the heights of Salisbury Plain gave various Victorian machineries all the power they needed. The river's name is possibly from the Old Norse *bisa,* meaning 'to strive'.

In trying to slip-slide and strive my way, toes first, into the flows of Elphame I've felt, in truth, nothing very much in the past few days. But as I stood on one particular bridge and watched the Biss's flow toward and beneath my feet from its source, due south of there, I had a flicker of presence I had not felt in a long time...

I must explain, without trying to tout one of my books.

Some years ago I was somewhat swamped by an energy, shaping as an entity, that I came to call 'du Lac'. I wrote about this du Lac (never using the poncy 'Lancelot' that he/it regarded as a slave name) in modern terms, setting his adventures in the present-day City of Bath. Which, I suppose in retrospect, was an entirely apposite place for someone called du Lac. I eschewed those prancing prats Galahad and Perceval and their sterile 'Virgins Only' obsessions with what I see as the un-Holy Grail. You know what I mean – that sanctified platter of spiritual plastic that enabled them to bugger off to eternal bliss and leave the rest of humanity to suffer. Not a notion or book to everyone's taste, I will admit, although I do think it was the best thing I've written. The sense of du Lac's energies swirled through our house for a few timeless weeks.

And then went.

One of the things that I learned from reading the old medieval descriptions of du Lac was that, inexplicably, he was sometimes described as almost having 'absences'. When he should have been charging at battlements or defeating foes, he just stood alone, staring, oblivious to the world around. There was no reason to build these into the storylines, yet I felt that, somehow, they touched upon something Faery.

So I think that we all have these 'moments'. Not any kind of entrancement or *petit mal,* but moments when a kind of unearthly, holy and almost child-like Stillness descends without warning, without reason; and while you're aware of the world and all its bustle, you're actually slightly removed from it at the same time. *Peace peace peace...*

So I had a 'du Lac' moment on the bridge as I stood over the River Biss, when I should have been walking briskly toward town. And after a few blinks that may have involved the birth and death of inward universes, I sent my thoughts up-current toward its source, where our extraordinary friend Una Woodruff lives, who knows more about faery and Elphame - and just about anything else you can imagine - than anyone I know. I think she might have got the message, because I got a nice long email from her that day.

So I suppose that for this document you're reading now I've ceased to be a researcher and have become a witness, a curator, a vessel.

That's sounds very clever but I got the whole sentence from the book by Terence Stamp that arrived yesterday and see, as I suspected, that there always was and hopefully still is, something inherently 'Other' about him. I suppose that I'm somehow, unseen to anyone in the outer world very light-heartedly 'Kneeling before Zod'!

I didn't get any spiritual messages while I stood on the bridge, but I think that Stillness itself is a form of communication, and the unexpected memory of du Lac was part of it. I did have an overwhelming vision of him once when undergoing a Quantum Healing session in Devizes. It healed nothing that I could feel, but I had a hypnogogic moment as I was coming out, of a huge, knowing, benign du Lac with golden eyes. I'll let you know if he re-appears during this piece of Work.

I finished Terence Stamp's slim book and strolled down the library to return it. An odd thing has been happening in this area. For the first time in anyone's memory/gnosis – in fact for the first time in recorded history - there is an alignment of the 3 Norths: Magnetic North, True North and Grid North. This started in 2014 at the tip of Cornwall, far to the west of here, and is slowly moving eastward across the country. It was, apparently, moving sideyways through Trowbridge at that very moment. As I stood on the bridge over the Biss I was, for once, aligned with the World and all its energies.

As for what must seem like my endless brisk walks to the library by diverse routes I should explain:

1. It is an excellent, large library and a community hub.
2. It is five minutes walk from home.
3. I do lots of 'brisk walking' as part of my rehab.
4. I desperately needed to see what colour the River Biss was.

Don't ask me why as to number 4. So I went back to the bridge again and saw that the flowing waters were greeny-black. Or were they blacky-green? With white flowing spurts of bubbles. I know that the tiny streams in this area that pour directly from the rocks at Luccombe's Bottom are crystal clear, purer than our tap water. But this was not pollution flowing beneath me, just the river carrying the rich substance of the soil with it. Green-black, black-green. With short flecks of silver-whiteyness, bubbles. I had read somewhere that when John Walsh, a healer from Netherbury in Dorset, was on trial for witchcraft in 1566, he said that there were three kinds of faery beings: white, green and black, each with their differing characters, not all of whom were congenial toward us humans. I'm summoning them now, flowing under my feet in a Wiltshire town. There are sirens behind me – Police, Fire or Ambulance? - I don't turn to look at these daily banshees with their differing roles, like Walsh's white, green and black fairies who also differed in their 'tones'.

This is not in any way a pretty or bucolic spot. It is an unexceptional bridge for light traffic in a run-down post-industrial town. Yet it had drawn me.

In my head I wrote a letter...

Dear John Walsh of Dorsetshire (as was)...What you must have gone through in 1566 after blabbing about the faeries! Were you being brave, confident, supported by local gentry or mad? Did they hang you or burn as a witch? I can't find out. You communed with the faeries in their barrows in the west of that magickal county. I only found a fragment of your life when I was googling something Zod had written: little more than a curled leaf of information, like the leaf I see swirling in a tiny vortex in the Biss below me. Yet you've given me, 457 years later, a tiny hint of Elphame in a Wiltshire town named after trolls.

I'm not arguing that this is a faery river. But I'm suggesting that for me, this is the flow of Elphame itself, and can be sensed in *every* land, though modified and shaped and coloured by the ancient myths of the Peoples.

Have I dipped into lecture mode?

I blame Stamp for this. There was something that he had written about Queen Mab that was spinning in the back of my mind like that leaf in the river. This was in the context of Shakespeare, in whom as an Ancient Brit I have little interest. Mab, he assured me, was a midwife in the faery realms, no bigger than a piece of agate. Mab. who helps sleepers give birth to their dreams, and was sometimes known as the Queen of Air and Darkness.

Many have argued as to her name. It can mean *child* or *son*. Or it came from 'Dame Habonde', a goddess who represents abundance, apparently associated with witches in Wales. "Customarily, people honoured Her on the first Monday in July by dancing around magical ritual fires whose smoke was said to purify both body and soul."

Softies argue that Mab was surely from Mabel, meaning lovable or dear, from the Latin *amabilis*, but that doesn't ring true to me. I can almost see Mab herself shaking her head on the far bank of the Biss, laughing. It was particularly a nickname for low-class women, or prostitutes, or hag-like witches. And Queen was also a pun on Quean, a term for prostitute.

Of those and many more, I prefer that last.

Perhaps the flowings of Elphame caused me to slip-slide into musing about the Colour Scales that were devised by Moina Mathers when they created the Order of the Golden Dawn. Would this greeny-black-whiteness fit within her kabbalistic scheme? *Vestigia Nulla Retrorsum* was my first Obscure Object of Magickal Desire when I was a teenager. She was next to me now, almost hippy-ish in that Slade Art School style I once found irresistable. She leaned forward, curious about the river.

NO NO NO... Don't get swirled away by Moina! I tell myself. Although any young man with a pulse would get hooked, Ancient Brits like I am now are a colder, more elusive sort of fish.

Mab Mab Mab...

Was there, in any part of Elphame, some combination of Black Goddess and Green Goddess who might be glimpsed in these waters?

Shortly after I left the bridge and strolled through town I had a curious encounter. It's funny how events and people that disappeared from my life twenty years ago can re-appear. I had assumed this person I met was submerged in some sort of stagnant dead-water in my subconscious, but she suddenly sprang out like a salmon to the lure, almost glistening.

I won't go into detail. It would be a tale told by a former eejit (me), signifying nothing at all to anyone else. But this former Neighbour From Hell who had given me endless torment had somehow been evoked to visible appearance and stopped me on the street. Things passed between us: a mutual and easy flow. She asked me for help in writing her own truly dark story. I gave it. Something odd trickled between us: kindness, forgiveness. I've never been good at the latter.

Was I being Mab, a midwife to her dreams and her future? Did Mab make me meet my former Neighbour from Hell? Or was it the Elphame-ish flow of the Biss? And is there a difference? Had I taken any other route or even this one seconds earlier or later, this wouldn't have happened.

I expect everyone has stories of this sort, though. I expect Mab is omnipresent.

Mab Mab Mab…

A gruesome thought just struck me. Zod described how Mab can appear as a small stone. At the moment I've got a small stone in my bladder that causes me to piss blood. Is this an aspect of Queen Mab within me having her period? Have I summoned her up? I'm not in any pain, and I'm having the stone removed soon, if my heart is strong enough.

Is that too gross for you? Maybe my urge to share is what caused Andro to blab the way he did.

I do have my own Faery Name, but that was chosen by my marvellous and uncanny wife. No-one else will ever learn it. I've always been curious about etymologies of places and people. When I was 'growing up' into the Western Mystery Tradition and drooling about Moina Mathers, aka *Vestigia Nulla Retrorsum*, I went through several of the Greek and Latin sort, all somewhat pompous. But if the *sidhe*, and all they are exist slightly to one side of us, vibrationally speaking, then the Faery Name must reflect this.

I say 'vibrationally speaking' as if I have some inside, technical knowledge of how these things work.

I. Do. Not.

I'm not even sure that makes sense. So here goes with another take...

In the 'olden days' that is to say in the 1950s onward when I was growing up physically but not obviously growing inward, it was possible to take a naff photograph with a Kodak Brownie camera. With a shaky hand focussing on a shaky subject, the print would come out blurry. (Is that what they mean by 'double exposure'? I think the latter was given as the reason for the Spirit Photographs that the Victorians put so much faith in.) In my case, it was almost as if two figures were overlapping slightly - both looking startled because I'd shouted at them to keep still when in fact it was my shaky hand. But imagine that the second, slightly overlapping/underlapping, blurry image is a parallel to your Faery self.

And this is what you must name.

Mab Mab Mab… even I'm not convinced by what I'm trying to say. I do recall that one of those accused of witchcraft in Scotland, Andro Man, explained how the Queen of his coven would take on any shape, becoming as old or young as she pleased. And someone else whispered that in this realm the Faery could appear as male or female as needs dictated. I'm reminded of *The Chariot* again. The more I look, the more the driver seems to be a female, and thus perhaps a manifestation of my *anima.*

Mind you, Andro Man of Aberdeen was probably a bit of a nutter. He spoke quite openly at his trial of having had 32 years of 'carnal relations' (nice old fashioned term for shags), and that she bore him many children.

He said all this in his trial in 1597. He was burnt in 1598. Was he just talking bollocks? You hear of people today pleading guilty to all sorts of heinous crimes with which they had no connection whatsoever. I'm sure there's a technical name for this. Did they do this for attention? Or are they simply fantasists who get swirled into a nonsense of False Memories? Andro Man would have known what his ultimate fate would be in that uncaring, unloving century. So did he truly believe in his Queen and her devilish partner? He had flair, no doubt about that, and spoke of how the Queen of Elphame rode on a white horse, and sometimes the Devil would appear out of the snow in the form of a white stag. I can almost see them, and I'm sure everyone reading this now will have just had a brief snapshot of this image.

White horse, Sacred Queen, Snow, Stag and Devil...

They were very big on the Devil in the 16th Century. Bizarrely, Andro's name for the Devil (or rather the Queen's partner) was Christonday. So I don't know what was going on there...

And Andro spoke of the children he created! I suppose these would be classed as Changelings. My dear friend Murry Hope always classed herself as a changeling, and that is how she named her autobiography. A changeling, don't ye know, was believed to be a faery that had been left in place of a human (typically a child) stolen by other faeries. Until I met Murry I always assumed this belief derived from horror and shame: when a woman gave birth to a baby that was deformed, disabled, or had what we now recognise as Down's Syndrome, they would tell neighbours that their true and perfect human baby had obviously been stolen by the faeries.

Murry was stunningly attractive in her last years, and equally but differently so when I tried to flirt with her 30 years earlier when she was a dark-haired Jacqueline Thorburn, founder of 'The Atlanteans'. Yet despite her five marriages – (I encouraged her to agree to the fifth with a *very* elderly fan of hers, for the financial security she desperately needed) - she was curiously a-sexual. More faery than human, I suppose.

Getting back to names and my quest for Elphame...

The Queen of Elphame, according to Northern English and Scottish sources, was NicNeven. That struck me as an odd name that doesn't sound right. I learned however that *Nic* is pronounced *Niss* and that opened various possibilities.

A **nisse**, from Nordic, specifically Danish folklore, is a gnome-like creature associated with the Winter solstice. It is still seen by some as a household spirit, and morphs across the storylines of north-west Europe (and hence presumably also North-eastern England and Scotland) into goblins or hobgoblins – whatever the latter might be. It might even be related to the *nixies* – shape-shifting water-spirits. In Denmark *nisser* are thought to be skilled in illusions and able to become invisible.

And staying with the Nordics, it is also felt that the Northern English Elfame or Elphame is from the Old Norse *Álfheimr.* Álfheimr was both the name of the supernatural world of the elves and the name of a kingdom whose legendary kings were related to the elves. All of whom were more handsome than any purely human people.

For some reason (and I must go with this mental flow, even if it irritates the reader) I remember in 1980 standing on a bridge looking down on the Monongahela River in Morgantown, West Virginia, where I lived for a time. Two hundred years before I stood there, the Monongahela River valley was the site of a sharp defeat for two thousand British and Colonial forces against those of the French and their Native American allies. 'The Mon' as they called it locally, is what you would call a *proper* river, compared with which the Biss is just a small piece of gently oozing dampness. I was in a personal torment that the powerful currents below me mirrored and seemed to magnify. I knew that my marriage was dead and that, marvellous though Morgantown was, I did not belong. The 'country roads and mountain mama' of West Virginia, in John Denver's lovely song, were never meant to be roads that *I* could travel. The Land did not speak to me, did not seem to want me. I was as lost as any of Andro Man's changelings must have been amid human folk. Not that I wanted to end it all by throwing myself in, but the angriness, coldness, swooshing, noisy bitterness of the waters matched my own internal state and there was an undeniable gravity.

Go home... The Mon compelled. *You will never belong here.*

A couple of years after that moment on the bridge in the US, I was in Jersey on the Channel Isle and Mike Nowicki 'saw' me as having had a past life in that West Virginia area and that time. Had I been picking up reincarnational echoes and/or something from my DNA that the flowing of The Mon unleashed? Or was it simply the Bridge itself - the liminality of being neither here nor there?

The dear little Biss, which is no more than a few yards wide and a couple of yards deep at its deepest, is little more than a rivulet of sweat on my brow. But with the help of Elphame, I was able to be in two places and eras at once, slip-sliding all over Time.

If there is such a thing as 7 Degrees of Separation, whereby I can, somehow, connect with everyone reading this, I think that this will hold true for Ideas as much as Persons. I struck me that because of Zod, I can almost instantly, like the flickering images I'd drawn in the corners of my daughters' book, summon up Madame Blavatsky. That means you can too. In fact you're doing it now – *flick flick flickering* with me.

How? Well, 'Zod' for me is little different to Madame Blavatsky's so-called 'Master' Koot Hoomi lal Singh. Whose real name, it seems, was Sirdar Thakar Singh Sandhanwalia, a founder of the 'Singh Sabha', whose aim was to reform Sikhism. No more than that. HPB, rather naughtily, took a real person in Indian politics and added a fictional slant; this morphed generations later into the 'Master Kuthumi' who sort of came alive, like Alexandra David-Neel's *tulpa* that you might want to Google.

So the fantastical Zod was as much of a creation as at least one (and probably all) of Blavatsky's 'Masters'. This enables me to slip-slide from Hollywood into the Himalayan mountain fastness of HPB's Thibet, taking in Krishnamurti (whom Terence Stamp really did know) and the dreadful phoney 'Bishop' Leadbeater along the way.

And if, according to Quantum Theory, there is no such Biss-like or Mon-like flow of Past and Future and Everything is all happening At Once, then surely everyone reading this now is all at One with me?

You, me and the fays.

And as you read this, whoever you are, you're flickering in my mind too. If it's not too late, and doesn't sound too weird, I think we should all send some powerful Queen of Elphame-ish thoughts toward poor Andro Man to sustain him until his execution. According to as much of Quantum Theory as I can understand: A particle can be in two places at once; Everything that can happen does happen; There are least 11 dimensions. So...

*Dear Andro... People centuries away are aware of you. The particles of our ideas are in two separate times, worlds apart, yet are with you in your head and heart and prison cell, and at the stake, instantly. All the madness that you're accused of, and which you talk about, **did** happen and **does** happen. Somewhere in the 11 dimensions is your own Elphame, and the Queen and Christonday send their love and are waiting for you. Perhaps **we** are the children you said you'd created?*

That's me trying to make sense of the insensible, so don't put too much weight on it. Though it strikes me that of course it's *not* too late! In the Quantum Realm there is no such flow as that we perceive as Time. Now I'm struggling... I must learn more.

Perhaps the simplest point of 'Elphame' is that it will always be to one side of anything logical, like that double-exposed person. largely invisible if not incomprehensible.

.

I know that we all have moments when Stillness descends and envelopes us. I was going to say ' moments when Time stops' but that is not quite the case.

Last weekend, on a picnic at Langford Lakes we found ourselves on a narrow, earthen path, between high, wild, madly-coloured planty things. (Forgive my ignorance of yet another aspect of this world I live in.) We found ourselves standing still, bewitched by clouds of dragonflies. Apparently the collective noun is 'odonoates' but that's ugly; these were *beeeee*autiful! I've done some research since and it seems these might even have been females of the species known as 'damselflies', with bodies thin as the thinnest of twigs, no more than two inches long. *Damsel* and *Flies*. Damsels Flying. Everyone a Witch Queen. Mabs and Nevens galore

These were the purest bolts of electric-blue, tiny witches' brooms of pure magick, doing things to the plants that we will never understand. There were so many of them, fluttering so fast that we couldn't see their shimmering wings or tiny body parts, just these minute electrickal witch-brooms or self-propelled wands if you prefer.

We kept quiet.

Still still still...

I presume *we* were invisible to *them* because we were so vast and slow, existing in irrelevant ways. There were a couple of other dragonflies further along by the crystal stream and these were a normal size, wings and limbs clearly visible, like pterodactyls in comparison to those around us. One of the larger ones winked at me in passing, but I'm probably making that up that.

(I met a man last week who was deeply into 'Otherness' with a wiccan slant. We swapped various 'Stillness' yarns. One of mine was in a grubby back alley near heavy traffic in the city of Bristol; his was in the fug of an underground station deep below the streets of London. My point being that Stillness can happen anywhere.)

The cloud of dragonflies stayed in our minds. Later, in an *out-of-time not-quite-earthly* Tea Rooms near Langford, the stillness still echoed, if that's not an oxymoron. We sat in the coolth and mused upon those films in which, using wonderful special effects, faery creatures danced and pranced and the Elven World was pure and impossibly perfect and you just wanted to ignore the popcorn and enter that realm forever. And that slid me into all those yarns by people with the Second Sight, able to see (what I imagine to be) the *real* thing.

Some of these yarns do bother me. I read a long piece recently about a woman in Ireland. She described her relationship with a leprechaun from Achill Island in the country of Ireland, who could have come out of Central Casting[1]. His name, he told Tanis Helliwell, was Lloyd. Now that's a fine Welsh name, derived from the Welsh word *llwyd*, which apparently means 'gray-haired' or even 'sacred'. While not typically associated with youth, gray hair is often interpreted as a symbol of wisdom and mature intellect. Lloyd is also a popular surname throughout parts of Wales, and it bothers me a little that an archetypal Leprechaun from the very westernmost coast of Ireland should give himself a purely Welsh name.

On the other hand I've suddenly got W.E. Butler sitting next to me, on my left side and thus right brain. I've known (of) him most of my life and he never seems to change: spritely, solid, powerful and bright. If you ever had to do the 'Harrowing of Hell' to rescue lost souls from Demons you'd want him to help. Or more simply, if you ever needed meaningful and healing contact with your 'dearly departed' you could be sure he had the psychic talents. I think he's somewhat intrigued by the comparative vastness of this very modern Atrium. Oh and by the way, if any readers have never heard of Walter Ernest Butler then no matter how many followers they might have on their blogs and vlogs and on-line Initiatory Courses, they are still only in the Outer Court.

He makes me realise that my daughters, born and bred in Wiltshire in England, have Greek, Gaelic, Chinese and Russian names, so maybe 'Lloyd' for a Leprechaun is not *so* unlikely.

Ernest, known to some as Cheiron, reminds me of an encounter he had with a fay somewhere in Hampshire, I assume. This fay was also from Central Casting (I forget the sartorial details, sorry) but Ernest asked the ethereal being to reveal its *true* form – as much as any Human mind could

---

1   *The Elemental Connection*, Nexus Magazine, April-May 2023.

gasp such a thing. And it transformed into a pulsation of shimmering light, almost geometric in pattern.

So maybe 'Lloyd' was simply shaping himself in a way that Tanis Helliwell could grasp. I think the energies behind *all* Inner Contacts do the same.

Well, I wanted to believe what the leprechaun was telling us Humans, even though much of it didn't make sense. Plus I've read too many books about modern day guru figures who just fibbed their way across and between the worlds and into our fancies, like Carlos Castaneda, Lobsang Rampa, C.W. Leadbeater and L. Ron Hubbard to name but four. I could go on, hugely... Then again, I suppose Elphame isn't *meant* to make sense.

Mr. Butler, I say, not daring to be presumptuous and call him Ernest. *Mr. Butler, what do you think about* – But he'd gone.

However, there is one yarn from someone whom I trusted completely. This was the late and much-lamented Canon Anthony Duncan, the immensely psychic priest from the Deliverance Ministry of the Church of England. He became aware that he shared his house with a faery being when said fay appeared and berated him for moving his furniture. Apparently it had a knock-on effect in the adjoining realm. In future, it was agreed between them, if Tony wanted to move his furniture drastically he would agree to negotiate with this co-existing Being of shimmering light!

I do this in our house. I act 'as if'. I pretend, though quietly, hopefully bothering no-one in this world or the adjoining one. Try it yourself but don't make a fuss.

There does seem to be a bewildering variety of 'Gentry' in Elphame, to use a term *They* seem to favour. To be honest, I'm still a bit bothered by the Lloyd's story, in which he uses the term 'Elementals' as we would 'Humans', and within the grouping he includes field fairies, pixies, trolls, goblins and elves as belonging to different Clans. To me, brought up into the Western Magical Tradition, elementals were creatures of Air, Earth, Fire and Water – Sylphs, Gnomes, Salamanders and Undines respectively. I'm not sure that Lloyd would agree. His story is about building bridges between the Human World and the

Elemental World. I'm all for that and will help in any way I can, but although Lloyd's story came to me unexpectedly in a 'meant to be' sort of way, it's still jarring at the moment. Then again, perhaps it is meant to; perhaps that unease is part of it; the uneasy mingling and clashing flows of the Black and Green with hints of Silvery-white. So I must become like a theatre-goer and 'suspend disbelief' to appreciate the actual energies of the players and not the artificial stage and scenery before which they perform.

Another day. As I cross the River Biss I notice it is particularly still, almost motionless. I can see an old grocery cart from the nearby ASDA supermarket lurking below the surface, and even I can't transform this into a legendary faery castle sunk beneath the waves. If I could reach it from the bank, and if I was young and full of alchemickal vims and vigours I'd try to remove it, even though no-one else is even aware of its existence. I'm sure there's symbolism in that.

But now I'm back scribbling this in the large Atrium of my local library, killing time until Dave the Roofer appears to sort out some leaky tiles and Jason the Broadbander to fix our signal. Suspending my own disbelief, this place is more fun than the legendary Reading Room of the British Museum where W.B. Yeats and McGregor Mathers and the somewhat elfin Moina would gather and create those Golden Dawns that are still rising and illuminating people today.

Hmm… those very words: *Reading Room of the British Museum.* For a bookish lad like me, and (among many other things) a former librarian, this is almost an invocation. That room summoned some of the greatest names in modern history...

Sun Yat-sen, Karl Marx, Oscar Wilde, Friedrich Hayek, Marcus Garvey, Bram Stoker, Mahatma Gandhi, Rudyard Kipling, George Orwell, George Bernard Shaw, Mark Twain, Vladimir Lenin (using the name Jacob Richter), Virginia Woolf, Arthur Rimbaud, H. G. Wells, Arthur Conan Doyle, Carl Jung... On and on. A Golden Horde of transforming writers. And did you know that in its heyday the Library provided a 'breakfast' that included champagne and ice cream laid out on the catalogue desks!

My own Atrium that bridges the Wiltshire Council offices and its bureaucracy with the lively community hub of the town's excellent Library, is an altogether more modest affair. It used to have a cafe and a restaurant, but Covid put a stop to both. Instead they've got an excellent vending machine and every time I have a cuppa from that I can feel myself under that *fin de siecle* British Museum Pleasure Dome of my dreamings.

Do the people in the Atrium of these local Council Offices realise that they're being ensorcelled by me? I mean, is that bearded chap arguing with an official about his tenancy an echo of Karl Marx? Is that troubled young chap texting furiously into his i-phone perhaps a continuation of Yeats, during those years when Maude Gonne gave him such grief by giving him nothing at all? You can see how horny and frustrated Yeats was for much of his adult life. And that fella on the phone is going to have a dreadful case of Tech Neck if he's not careful.

I realise that I'm surrounded by a variety of Humans as bewildering and different in their elemental needs as anything that Lloyd described for his Elemental Realms. In my mind, the legendary British Museum Library and this entirely modern Atrium are overlapping.

Blink. Blink. Blink. Say things three times.

Ernest… what do you think about Elphame?

But he'd gone.

Then...

BOO! HELLO ALAN!

I had no sooner finished scribbling the above paragraphs when an old friend and work-mate surprised me. I will call her 'Lucy, which means 'Light'. She had taken a detour through the Atrium on a happy impulse. If she had taken a different turn, or came through a tad later, we would never have met. We yarned for ages, but it was only after she departed that I realised something odd....

Lucy had just finished a long walk from the source of the River Biss in Upton Scudamore, following it to where it joined the River Avon on the outskirts of Trowbridge. It was not the best walk she had ever done, and took her through many skanky parts, but she felt compelled to do it. I realised that in many ways Lucy was a manifestation of the themes and impulses that seem to be driving this manuscript of mine: her passion for the Spirit of Place and the *genius locii* of Wiltshire; her work with the vulnerable, rejected people (Changelings?) in remote parts of the county; her knowledge of the strange alternative energies that flow through and beneath Frome; her agelessness. My long standing joke in the 20 plus years I've known her is that she never ages and so has clearly sold her soul to the Devil. Oh how we laugh! I don't think she ever rides a white horse like the Queen of Elphame, but Wiltshire is known as the County of White Horses, because of the numerous hill carvings of such. Her fella isn't actually called Christonday but his name is weirdly significant, though I will never blab. Lucy, who shares my passion for Ordnance Survey Maps, will never read this because she has no interest in my 'otherly' writing. Yet her whole life at the moment manifests the spirit of Elphame. I would suggest that Lucy was – is – a 'continuation' of its Queen, whereas I am somewhat loose within the worlds. And I would insist: We. All. Are.

The point of me describing this meeting is driven in part by my self-indulgent pleasure at an unexpected encounter with an old friend (I've never been good at the 'friend thing'), but mainly to insist that these patterns **happen to you also**, wherever you live, however you progress in your own Quest. There are currents in your life that may seem like trivial trickles to outsiders, but are actually cosmic flows. Child of Earth you may be, but you're treading through Starry heavens.

(I can't remember who said that first.)

As I get even older my thoughts step back between the Ageing Now and the Land of the Ever Young that exists, in a linear sense, nearly 7 decades before this. When I see young parents with their tiny children I feel... almost... I suppose *broody* if that's the right word. I look and think *I was that toddler; I was that young Dad.* Much as I love my grandchildren all equally, it is not quite the same. I'll have to think on this. Perhaps 'brood' is not the right word. Is this something to do with my inner Queen Mab?

I often flow back to that moment when I was 5, just started at Infant School, and Time and its World stopped as I became benignly possessed by an ancient Being, feminine in nature, who seemed to push little 'me' to the back of my skull and looked out toward my sister playing hockey in the yard for the Big Girls. Whoever, Whatever this Being was, she seemed to approve of my progress so far. Was this Mab, or NicNeven? I've never tried to give Her a name before. Definitely female in tone and ancient, utterly ancient. I always assumed that this was my Higher Self/Overself/*Ba* and so on... I always used these terms as though I were on intimate terms with them, but really it's just a clutchable concept, quite meaningless. This happened several times after that at long intervals, as I've written about elsewhere.[2] It was always a pleasant state, pure and comforting, this 'stopping the world' as I think Castenada called it rightly, even if he was a phoney.

Grow *with the* **flow** *Al*, says a voice on my right side and from my left brain. I turn.

Timothy! Good to see you. Sorry about last time.

---

2   *The Google Tantra.* Later edition re-titled *Sex and Light.*

Leary is looking a lot healthier in spirit (or is it just my mind?) than he had done in his last days.

I should explain that in the course of the babbling brook of the *might-have-beens, could-have-beens* and possibly *should-have-beens* of my life, I was supposed to visit him.

Laura Jennings, the hierophant of the 'Ra-Horakhte' Golden Dawn temple, had once been, she told me, one of his affectionately-termed 'Holy Women'. When I did a series of lectures in Seattle in the mid-90s she planned for us to fly down and stay with him. In her estimation, Leary was a true magician and she felt we'd get on well. In the event he had to cancel as he'd just been diagnosed with the cancer that would soon kill him.

I've never taken LSD or indeed any drug stronger than a few disappointing tugs on a reefer in Kentucky where, they wickedly assured me 'they roll their own'.

(This was a nod to it being a vast tobacco-growing state, but mainly a schoolboy-ish reference to the inbreeding that was apparently rampant in the isolated communities of Appalachia. They didn't think I'd understand, being a mere Limey. They were surprised when I did; I also explained exactly why the Hillbillies would always wear wellies (known to them as gum-boots) when they fancied shagging sheep instead of their sisters. I went up a lot in their estimation from then, and they even gave me toothpicks to chew on.)

However, I was always intrigued by reports of the 'gratuitous grace' that LSD users often described. I wondered if that was akin to those benign possessions I used to experience when young, though I wouldn't have taken any kind of drug to test this. Plus beyond that, I was always drawn to reading about the purely visionary possibilities of the drug, enabling the Second Sight in ordinary folk so they could 'see' as Mr. Butler and Æ and Yeats and even young Tanis Helliwell 'saw'.

I think that this non-meeting with Leary in L.A., as I recall, was another 'meant to be' moment. Or should I invert this to read: 'this meeting was a **not** meant to be moment.'

You're amused, Tim.

(Note the informality with him that I wouldn't use with **Mr.** Butler)

It's because, Al, things happen without you seeing. It's not a matter of chemicals or psychism.

Eh? Patterns? I suggested. *Like predictable ripples when flowing water hits a prominent rock?*

He chuckled.

Oh man, you are trying too hard to find new metaphors. Yeats hoped his spirits would bring them.

Yes, in his incomprehensible book 'A Vision'. The spirits told him: 'We've come to bring you new metaphors for poetry'. A continuation of Yeats is over there now, getting new metaphors from his iPhone.

Cool! But Al, our Universe has innumerable 'scripts' for which we provide the actors. Everyone will at some point re-enact one or more of the great mythic scripts. It doesn't mean they will become avatars or reincarnations of the figures involved, but 'Continuations'.

I might have/could/should have said more but I had a sudden thought that broke the **flow** I was trying to **grow** with, to use his own rhymed advice. At that moment, in that particular play, Who was **I** a continuation of?

I would have asked him; although his famous mantra was 'Turn On, Tune In, Drop Out', with me he had just Turned Up, Tuned In and now Buggered Off.

I *am* glad I didn't get to meet him. I see him as an interesting chappy but never one of my Heroes. Besides he kept calling me 'Al', and I've never liked being named after one of Aleister Crowley's books.

He must have triggered something within me because...

Bloody hell! If the Queen of Elphame and Christonday enacted a 'continuation' on me via Lucy, then *Who* am I? The only possible answer is that I'm a continuation of Andro Man! Remember him?

Andro Man blabbed in court (as Prince Harry is doing at this very moment), telling all sorts of things which may or may not be true, and which will lead him to the stake. Am I destined to be a Continuation of this? I've got a hefty op coming up soon to get rid of the Mab Stone that is worrying me a bit.

Some sources give his name as Andrew but I suspect they're being a bit superior. Both Andro and Andrew mean something like 'Manly'. So he was a Manly Man. Everyman? (The name 'Alan' by the way, means

Harmony, Handsome or Stone. That damned Stone again! Just saying. Sometimes these things matter.)

I suppose I should now give Andro Man's story as much as anyone knows it, if only to clarify his role in my mind and now in my life…

Andro claimed that he first met his Faery Queen when he was a boy. She appeared at his mam's house suddenly *'where she was delivered of a bairn.'* Man was kind to her and brought her water. In return, the faery promised him *'He should know all things and should be able to cure all sorts of sickness...'*

Who could refuse an offer like that!

He didn't meet her again for another 28 years, when he found her bewitching his cattle on a piece of land called 'Elf Hillock'. When she realized who Man was, the Queen apologized and they became lovers. The Queen also gave Man the power to steal milk from cows, divine the future and increased his ability to heal.

I'd certainly have gone along with that.

From that time onwards, Andro became known as a healer and 'cunning man', practising a kind of sympathetic magic to effect his cunning cures. One involved passing a patient through a hasp of unwashed wool nine times. A cat then followed nine times through the same hasp (so it could pick up the ailment). The cat was then killed, destroying the disease and so curing the patient.

I couldn't do the cat killing but the rest of the theory seems sound. Andro would probably be a homeopath these days.

Yet what about the Queen's fella, Christonday? Did Andro not worry about cuckolding a Horned God!

Well, there might have been a Crowleyan or Learyan touch about Christonday, because he didn't seem to mind being cuckolded – presumably for the greater good. The Queen, Neven, was probably just one of his 'Holy Women'.

If Andro wanted to summon him he simply used the word *'Benedicite'*, which is a blessing, or grace, and lo! He would appear.

I must try that.

I just did.

Three times.

Sitting in my garden office.

I'll let you know...

Andro explained to the court that while he may have been the Queen's vigorous lover, the mighty Christonday was his actual Master. According to him this was because: *"The queen has a grip of all the craft, but Christonday is the gudeman [husband] and so has all power under God."*

I keep reading Andro's answers to his Scottish Inquisitor (for that's exactly what the wretch was) and it's like Prince Harry in the High Court yesterday, facing down The Mirror. Never argue with Mirrors of any kind, I'd have warned both. I don't think either of them had been best advised.

His magic seemed entirely innocent. He harmed no-one and healed many. Thanks to the faeries he provided cures for human and animal diseases; helped find lost or stolen items; gave occasional glimpses of the future and no-one seemed to mind that he had sexual relationships with them. But daft, trusting Andro blabbed about the faeries to the wrong people, and that was his downfall.

It seems that there was a time in Catholic Scotland when faeries were **not** equated with demons. Confessing to contacts was not so bad, and Andro's cures were applied whilst invoking the Holy Trinity. Under this Catholic church, although faeries were hardly 'approved' of, they were not explicitly evil or demoniacal. Those priests even had a notion that the fays might – just might - be fallen angels. Maybe in Andro's mind the actual name of his Master, 'Christonday', was something of an insurance policy when it came to the priests who quizzed him.

For the common folk who were Andro's patients and customers, the faeries were fundamentally part of the Christian universe. However, when Protestantism prevailed across most of Britain, it brought a far more literal approach to the Bible, particularly in Scotland. As a result women were often treated as criminals, through prosecutions for scolding, prostitution and of course the inevitable suggestion of Witchcraft. Those miserable scunners (you might want to google that word) discouraged plays and poetry that were not devotional in nature; and to their mind, while faeries are not mentioned in the Guid Book, demons are. Therefore, faeries **have** to be demons.

You can almost see Andro's new-fangled Protestant questioner doing the slimy Good Cop thing like some of the car salesmen I've known (especially that wretch who sold me a dodgy Peugeot 104 in 1986). I think that's why he was so unguarded. To that unholy lot, his naive and sentimental talk of the faeries stank of sulphur and brimstone. His descriptions of feasting and cavorting with beings with the '*shapes and claithes like men*' who could never the less appear '*out of the straw in the likeness of a staig*' (a young male horse) smacked of a witch's Sabbath.

And so, no doubt to his astonishment and at a time when he was still invoking his faery Master with the surely acceptable name of 'Christonday', he was duly convicted of witchcraft and subsequently burnt.

Unholy Bastards, all of them, Prods *or* Catholics.

Benedicite, Benedicite, Benedicite... I hope you were there for him, Christonday. Don't bother coming near me if you weren't.

L ast night a cohort of witches flew above our street. All of our neighbours saw them, and indeed the whole town. Look for yourself in yesterday's on-line *Wiltshire Times* (8/6/23) if you don't believe me. The roaring, the rolling thunder, the sense of pure, unadulterated evil, the black cloaks trailing to points, the sharp noses that sliced through the Aires, the rattling of their bones and the dark powers they projected that made all our skins crawl and fear for the future. War and Rumours of Wars and Ghost Riders in the Sky, no doubt.

All right, all right I concede that the *Wiltshire Times* explained these away as merely USAF B1 Lancer bombers (nicknamed 'Bones' from B-One), on their way to RAF Fairford in nearby Gloucestershire, but in the atmospheres invoked by dear and doomed Andro, I know what they *really* were.

I've heard nothing from Christonday despite the invoking words I used. Then again, maybe that was the true cause of the Bone Witches yesterday. I've still got Andro Man in my head and I think that I might be 'continuing' him in a small and hopefully harmless way.

I'm actually scribbling this in a different sort of Atrium today. In this case, that of the Royal United Hospital where I'm about to get my preliminary Medical Interview to see if I'll be fit enough (after last year's heart attack) to have the Mab Stone removed. I suppose in a small way it might parallel Andro's own Inquisition: we both have to give honest answers to personal and indeed intimate questions; we both have to have all sorts of tests. I doubt if he, as a male, will be searched for the supernumerary nipple that was seen a sure mark of a Witch, but I know that apart from blood tests, ECG's and urine samples I will also have to be swabbed in my throat and crotch.

I don't mean to make fun of, or try to diminish, what he went through by making this probably risible comparison. But he is in my head, and I can't help thinking that his detailed confessions seemed remarkably incautious and even somewhat unworried.

With my lifelong and usual Time-anxieties I got the train in and arrived here two hours before needed. But the RUH is effectively a large village or even a small town with shops and cafes and filled with helpful people and an underlying sense of the hopefulness I feel in all our NHS hospitals. I've been coming to this place for many health issues (mainly my hearing) for 40 years now.

Scribble scribble scribble. Andro Andro Andro...

There is a large vending machine next to me. It has buttons for several varieties of coffee, hot chocolate, mocha (whatever that is) black tea, white tea, and a couple of buttons for Moët & Chandon and Montrachet Grand Cru.

I might be imagining the last two.

B listering heat for the past few days, and I struggle with hot heat. I take after my Dad in that respect. On the rare occasions we got days like that in Northumberland he'd swelter and say: 'Ah divvn't like it man, it's wick, really wick' which I always took to mean 'wicked'. The older I get, the more I find myself taking after him, and perhaps understanding him a bit better. Must be the DNA thing. And the weather really has been wick for me – I'm not sure if Geordies still use that term.

I'm scribbling in 'my' Atrium again, the one attached to the Library. It's filling up with the University of the Third Age, or U3A as they code themselves. They have a weekly walking group for the elderly (i.e. mostly younger than me). I'm usually too busy head-down scribbling (or pretending to scribble) to see if they have a particular leader. I say 'pretend' because I'm afraid that they might ask me to join them. I'd always decline, but with thanks, as I'd have to talk to people en route. The various engaging, socially adept, charming personas of my once Satanic charm have been put to one side. Maybe when I get the Mab Stone removed and my heart muscles stronger I'll be up for it.

They've just launched themselves beyond the doors with what seems like a kind of hive consciousness. Perhaps I should associate them with the Wild Hunt. You know – the spirit riders that gather up lost souls, usually from sacred hills, and carry them 'on' into the Light and Peace. I did something like that on Cley Hill once, when I was in me prime. Made my nape hairs prickle as I came down from on high with the spirits behind me:

Don't Look Back Don't Look Back Don't Look Back...[3]

The Atrium is almost empty now except for an elderly but very vigorous man wearing a formal light-brown suit that rather hangs off his

shoulders where he has lost weight with age. I reckon it would have fitted him handsomely when he was young and in his ursine prime. I strikes me that he is rather like me in my clothes at the moment. After the heart attack last year I still haven't recovered the weight I lost from my finely sculpted body. (I might be exaggerating about a finely sculpted body. And I was never ursine.) He was smoking his large pipe very happily. The staff

---

3   See my essay about Cley Hill in my *Short Circuits*.

40

on the reception desk can't fail to see him, yet none come bustling across to throw him out, or just tell him firmly but politely that smoking is NOT allowed.

He winks at me.

It's not really a pipe and there's not really any tobacco in it.
Is there any point to that?
I helps you connect. It's how you always saw me.
Why should I connect?
Because you're always quoting me. I've been in your head for a long time. Look through your own memories and dreams and reflections.
That's absurd.
The highest truth and greatest absurdity are one and the same.
You're right Dr. Jung. I'll quote that one too.

I had a greatly absurd thought. The good Doctor could see it ripple.
Go with the flow junger Mann...

What if that group of people I had assumed was the 'University of the Third Age' was a bit a like your pipe and tobacco – a means for my imagination to connect? What if it really **WAS** the Wild Hunt?!

What if they ask me to join them?

Tell them you're not ready. Banish them, as they banished the Banshee that so terrified you as a boy.

The Banshee...

I haven't lost track of the Land of Elphame, but I find this heat doesn't let me flow into it. I don't even want to go and stand on the bridge over the Biss and try for any equivalence. Instead I have an absurd memory from my childhood that Dr. Jung advised me to go with, so bear with me.

Last night, probably on *Facebook*, someone asked people for the most terrifying movie they had ever seen. Depending on your age, you can imagine the titles that appeared. For me, the one film that evoked pure and primal terror was not *The Exorcist,* or *Texas Chain-Saw Massacre* etc etc etc etc etc etc etc... it was the Disney film I saw in the cinema at the age of 7, called:

Darby O'Gill and the Little People.

It was meant to be a light-hearted, wholesome family jaunt involving a *very* young Sean Connery and a cute leprechaun exactly like the one called Lloyd. And so it was, but the scenes involving the Banshees had me curled into a foetus on the seat with my Mam trying to reassure me and persuade me to open my eyes and stop shaking.

It's aall richt, pet, aall richt...

I mentioned the 'DNA thing' earlier. I've only recently stumbled on the fact that my maternal ancestors only lived in Scotland as a stop-gap. In fact they came over from Killally in County Cavan, in Ireland, at the time of the Great Famine.

I know it might seem to be stretching it a bit, perhaps as an attempt to excuse my wimpiness in the Wallaw Cinema, but I *knew* about those Banshees as soon as the name was mentioned. Was that a DNA Memory, as many people have discussed?

> **Banshee** *bean sí*, 'woman of the fairy mound' or 'faery woman'. A female spirit in Irish folklore who heralds the death of a family member, usually by screaming, wailing, shrieking, or keening.
>
> Or she may be seen at night as a shrouded woman, crouched beneath the trees, lamenting with a veiled face; or flying past in the moonlight, crying bitterly: and the cry of this spirit is mournful beyond all other sounds on earth, and betokens certain death to some member of the family whenever it is heard in the silence of the night

Those bits above are from Wikipedia. But at the age of 7 I already *knew* all that. In the decades since I have sat through all sorts of terrifying movies without turning a hair, because at the back of my mind I knew what *real* terror was. In fact it was only a couple of years ago that I bought the DVD of *Darby O'Gill* and was able to watch the whole sequence and see exactly what it was that I dared not look upon, the screaming terror I *already* understood from the ancestral depths of

Ireland, that need not speak it's name because I knew it – *Bansheeeeee...*!

So I'm quite certain that our ancestors are not dead and gone. They are buried in every gene, every cell of our DNA. And maybe I'll find the Land of Elphame via that route.

Oh that's a bit overdramatic, isn't it? I blame the heat. It's wick.

B listering sun again. It's still wick. To avoid the worst of the heat later on and still get in the 10K steps I need, I went into town much earlier and by a different route. I was swamped by wave after wave of children going to their two different and rival secondary schools, their contrasting uniforms a curious melange of the faery colours - green and black, with flashes of white. Their schools named after Saints.

It was like wading into the past, heading into the sources of my own childhood and the dread I felt most mornings. Or should I reverse the imagery and say I felt like a fixed rock in the Biss, feeling the memories from the Source scouring from my Past toward my Futures?

Didn't they know **Who** I am!?

Listen, children, I am the incarnation of every kind-cruel, weak-strong, bright-dark, hard-soft, hopeful-despairing, fearful-fearless impulse you have ever had or ever will have. I am YOU! I am ALL. But which of those noisome, bullet-headed, semi-human little scrotes in particular would become my co-walker or double? (Of which more in a moment, because I'm sure I caught a glimpse of Robert Kirk in the shadows where I should have been walking, on the other side of the road.)

I read somewhere that the faery realm was created in parallel with ours, but the fays themselves had no free will, and had a hive mentality. These lot flowing around me had no free will either – they *had* to go to school. And they were certainly in their own swarms, buzzing incomprehensibly. A few brushed against me; some made micro-apologies. Of course, I was the Invisible Man; some old git - or gadgy, as my Dad would say – getting in their Way.

And so many of them were doing unfathomable things with their phones, scrying into them, listening intently with their heads tilted slightly to one side like mediums when they receive messages from the dead. I suppose such devices are manifestations of their Higher Selves. Maybe I should give my own phone a name. Instead of naming my ugly, over-large-but-cheap device from Tesco as *Overself* or *Ba* maybe I'll get a better signal from Above if I call it *NicNeven*. That's worth a try.

This bridge over the Biss is different to the one I've been describing so far. That other one overlooks two Pizza take-aways and a shop for quality Sandwiches. Here, from one angle, the area is actually quite pretty with a squat stone Victorian lock-up (i.e. prison for drunks), a small weir, viewing area and occasional swans. That's if you look at it from one side. On the *other* side of the road it all dissolves into a ruined factory-site that has yet to be redeveloped and probably never will be in my lifetime. I suppose that's also a metaphor for life. When I get to be a millionaire from this Scratch Card I've got in my heart pocket I'll build an ice-rink on the site and get another fortune and probably a knighthood.

I'm somewhat troubled by these swirlings as the drop of the weir makes them quite strong. I've been kept thinking about Christonday, because I was startled by stumbling upon a certain Marion Grant, also of Aberdeen, who was tried in 1597 for her contacts with the faery man she also called Christonday. There can't be two such Beings with such an oddity of a name, can there? According to her story, presumably wrung by torture, Christonday had come to her and asked her to call him Lord and become his servant - to which Marion consented. They had, one imagines, vigorous and satisfying sexual intercourse every month. She admitted that she worshipped him on her knees and that he had taught her healing powers in return.

Marion also got burned at the stake. Whether at the same time as Andro Man I don't need to know.

But I wonder if Marion had betrayed Andro, because the Inquisitors came after him the following year, and the story of him tupping the Faery Queen of Elphame over 30 years and producing 30 babies all came pouring out. And, I learned further, his sign of his commitment to his Queen was that every year on Rood-day he would kiss her 'airss'.

Well, I can't mock him for that. If the young Moina Mathers asked me when I was young and single to kiss her airss, I'd have done it on any and every day of the year and not just the 14th of September.

I realise that's twice now I've stumbled upon this Christonday, the Faery King. To paraphrase Ian Fleming, Once is chance, twice is coincidence, but a third time I will take as Enemy Action and act accordingly.

I'll let you know.

Andro Andro Andro...Marion, Marion, Marion... Peace Peace Peace.

When I think about their harmless but helpful lives and their truly fiery ends, I really must stop whining about this summer's heat as it's really quite lovely now that I've put on shorts and feel like a boy again.

I don't want to get sucked down into the whole history of the Witch Trials that were such a blemish on our history. Millions of words have been expended on discussing Who or What the witches were connecting with – if anything or anyone. Were the fay separate, physical Beings? Were those Witches what we would now call psychic mediums connecting with spirits? Were the spirits inter-dimensional energies? Or fallen angels as some would argue?

I don't want to get drawn and perhaps drowned by diving into such vortices, as I've read enough about all of these in the past and still have no clear conclusions.

Still at the bridge... There's quite a strong flow from this one.I'm not at all surprised to feel Mr. Butler behind my left shoulder, peering over.

Ehyeh Asher Ehyeh he whispers over the waters.

Eh? It's not often you hear Hebrew uttered on a bridge in a town named after Trows.

It used to be translated as 'I Am that I Am'. But it's perhaps more accurate to translate it as 'I am the Ever-becoming One'.

So that's me? Ever-Becoming, like the River?

It's everyone. All rivers. Everything is connected. All the worlds.

Dr. Jung told me that we all retain traces of an existence which isn't earthly.

Elphame, you mean.

A fire engine roars past, blue lights and sirens clawing at the air. One of my daughters, the gentlest of women, is a fire-fighter and has the awesome powers that control such a beast. For an infinite micro-second of non-time I am at her birth on a blistering hot day like this in the city of Bath, once known as Aquae Sulis, marvelling at her progress since, at every stage, ever-becoming.

I turn. The bridge is empty.

I had hoped to get away from the grim whirlpool of the Witch Trials but I'm still circling the vortex. What is the name of that whirlpool in the Hebrides? Corry....er...vrekan? Yes, that's it. Corryvrekan. Third largest whirlpool in the world. Caused by a 'Sea Witch' – lovely concept that! - but named after a lovelorn Norwegian Prince who failed in a test set by his potential father-in-law. Marine scientists have revealed that the whirlpool is actually caused by a giant rock pinnacle that rises from the ocean bed, but what do they know, eh? It's clearly the work of a Sea Witch and I won't hear any different.

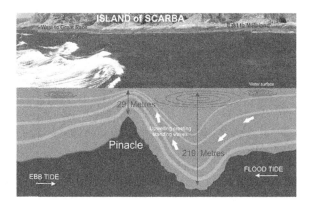

I would never dare go near such a thing; I'm quite sure that I've had at least one past life in which I drowned. Long, irrelevant stories those are!

I've learned that the Scottish Parliament apologised and pardoned all those guilty of the 'crime' of witchcraft on 8 March 2022. How did I miss that?

That makes me feel a bit better about Andro and Marion. I thought that if I got the names (powerful things, Names) of all the victims I would do a little witchy thing of my own below the Moon, in our long and narrow garden, in the area where we encourage our own 'Gentry'. I assumed it might only have been a couple of dozen, but it turned out that an estimated 4,000 to 6,000 people, mostly from the Scottish Lowlands, were tried for witchcraft during a major series of trials in 1590–91, 1597, 1628–31, 1649–50 and 1661–62. More than in any other country in Europe. Seventy-five per cent of the accused were women. The very last person to be executed was poor Janet Horne at Dornoch in 1727, who had been jailed with her own daughter.

As I tried to find out actual names, I clicked myself into the Akashic Records (known to me as the *World Wide Web,* and believe you me far more informative than anything the famed 'Halls of Akasha' have ever revealed). As I did so I kept getting the name 'Bessie Dunlop' from Wikipedia, and thankfully there was not the slightest hint of Christonday.

So indulge me while I make a brief visit, because the Wikipedia entry also has photographs of the entrance to Elphame!

When Bessie Dunlop was accused of sorcery and witchcraft she answered her accusers that she received information on prophecies, the whereabouts of lost goods and natural healing remedies from Thomas Reid, a former barony officer of Blair near Dalry who claimed to have been killed at the Battle of Pinkie some 29 years before in 1547. She described him in terms of an elderly, well dressed, honest and respectable man with a long grey beard who carried a white wand, and revealed to her interrogators that she had *Never known him when he was alive.*

(I do like the sound of that. Very few self-professed modern magicians and warlocks and witches, for all their noises and hints, actually have that sort of power.)

Bessie asked Thomas why he was being so kind to her during a difficult time. He answered that he had been ordered to help her by the Queen of Elphame. It transpired that at the time of Bessie's recent labour a stout lady had come to her door seeking a drink and this was none other than the Queen herself. A drink had been provided and this element brings various traditional folklore aspects into the equation such as a changeling child, as hers was sickly; both she and Thomas predicted the wee bairn's death, as well as the recovery of her poorly husband.

Near where she lived in the hamlet of Linn, in Ayshire, were (and are) the caves known as the 'Elfhame o' the Blair' or the 'Elfhouse', and the locals at that time believed that these magical creatures had made this their abode within the many chambers containing stalactites and stalagmites. At Halloween it was said they would come riding out of the caves on horses that were the size of mice, their long yellow hair streaming or tied in knots with crimps of gold. Their 'quaichs' or friendship cups, were acorn cups and they drank wine beneath the toadstools. Their clothes were green velvet and their arrows were made of moss-reed tipped with flint arrow heads that were dipped in hemlock poison. The bows were made from the rib bones of unbaptised babies who had been secretly buried in the shaws and glens. It is not known how old these 'Elfhame' traditions are, however excavation shows that it had been dwelt in by early man but had been used by Covenanters seeking a hiding place from the king's troops.

I had to Google 'Covenantors'. It seems they were ardent supporters of the Presbyterian Church, their faith being based on the teachings of those miserable, joyless entities John Calvin and John Knox. Their name comes from the National Covenant of 1638, an oath to resist the attempts by Charles I to introduce a new Prayer Book in Scotland. After the 1660 Restoration, the Covenanters lost control of the Kirk and became a persecuted minority, leading to several armed rebellions and a period from 1679 to 1688 known as 'The Killing Time'.

Well, I can only hope that the Covenanters being persecuted were of the same persuasion as those who tortured Bessie using the methods that are recorded but I don't want to detail. I hope the bastards suffered dreadfully.

She was taken to the High Court of Justiciary in Dalkeith 20 September 1576. On 8 November she was found guilty and sentenced to be strangled and then burnt on Castle Hill in Edinburgh.

Bessie Bessie Bessie… Peace Peace Peace…

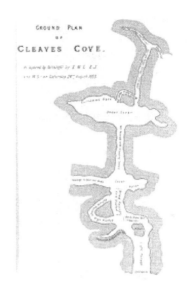

Above left, is a photo of the entrance to a localised Elphame. On higher quality images I can almost fancy a wraith looking out. On the right is the internal lay-out, with chambers named as Court, Great Court and Glittering Rock. I dare say it's the sort of thing you can create a path-working for, though I don't like doing such things these days.

That description of Bessie's Elphame is ridiculous. Bizarre. Incredible. Unbelievable. Against all evolutionary laws. I won't, however, reject it. I need to suspend disbelief because these match similar tales over the centuries across just about all the lands where faery lore exists. I won't sit here and say 'that can't possibly be true'; I *will* tell myself that in the quantum universe, everything that can happen does happen. We are tuned into the frequency that corresponds to our own physical reality; but there are an infinite number of parallel realities co-existing with us.

I'm not in any way trying to 'explain away' those minute creatures riding on horses the size of mice. I just have to accept that oddities happen that might never be understood, though I wouldn't mind 'Lloyd's' take on it. You can see that 'suspension of disbelief' is a powerful tool, although possibly a cop-out in my case.

There is one other possibility…

When I first read about the Roman Invasions of Britain and those Celtic lands that the Legions burned and slashed and tortured their ways across to civilise us, I was annoyed by the sniggering comments made by their commentators. I forget their names. I suppose you'd think of them as embedded journalists, out for a story or two. According to them, apart from tattooing ourselves until we were blue and silly, and wearing trousers instead of skirts like 'civilised' people did in Rome - oh and keeping severed heads of enemies, we hadn't a clue about the Facts of Life.

But pause here…

Picture yourself today in Louisville or Liverpool. Picture a group of mature women having a girl's night out, on the razzle, full of liquor, lusty talk and laughter, having fun in their favourite club/bar/nightclub. A stranger enters. A male. Dressed oddly. Weirdly. He speaks English haltingly and explains that he is from a far country and is here to learn the customs of this one. He has a large note pad and also a recorder. He can pay for the time. Although he is nervous he is clearly determined and utterly harmless.

You can see what happens. You don't need any remote viewing or far memories. The women's faces light up. This is too good an opportunity. So, they tell him the most ridiculous things, straight-faced. He has no sense of irony or any observable humour; he remains unaware they are taking the piss. Scribble scribble scribble… His words will last two thousand years.

I think that Native British women did exactly that with the Naive Roman chroniclers. Of course, the women knew *exactly* how babies were made, and what their periods were for, and the importance of that horrible spermy stuff the men had, that so resembled crushed mistletoe berries. Nothing to do with Moonlight on their bare stomachs and all the other guff they fed him with…

And so I wonder if – perhaps - something similar happened in remote parts of Britain and Ireland when posh fellas like Sir Walter Scott hitched up their carriages in remote places and asked the locals about these damn'd Faeries they'd been hearing about. I'd have told some cracking yarns myself, in those circumstances. People say I still do.

Just come back from the dentists. That whole question of the tiny critturs of the Elphame in Ayrshire was still bothering me. As my dentist probed and prodded and filled, I had Mr. Butler in my mind, for my thoughts seemed to have curled into a question mark that perhaps only he could straighten.

You've got a very small mouth, Mr. Richardson, said the dentist.

No-one had ever said that to me before. Quite the opposite. But I had an image of that small Elphame cave to match my own open maw.

*You know **an** answer*, said Mr. Butler, *Though it can never ever be **the** answer.*

Of course. I remembered his account of the faery being when he asked it to reveal itself in its truer form: a shimmering pulsation of almost geometric patterns.

If the person who had observed the Ayrshire faeries pouring out of the cave had done the same, he most likely would have seen them as they were truly were: waveforms and particles of energy, flowing and riding currents of the night and starlight.

So...

A modern scientist, blessed with the Second Sight (and my late friend Murry Hope knew several), would see what emerged from the cave mouth at Halloween as waves and particles.

A medieval farmhand would see this as little beings pouring from the mouth of the cave on mouse-sized horses.

Make another appointment Mr. Richardson, said the dentist, probably glad to escape from the narrow confine within my head.

I've tried to get away from this particular area – both geographical and mythical – but that image of the cave is potent. I'd advise you to Google 'Elphame Cave Ayrshire' and also the Images for 'Cleeves Cove' – to have a closer look at one image in particular, in colour. Of course, there is an obvious and raw vaginal power to it, especially with the red traceries (ochre?) on the outer lips. Physically it is part of a limestone cave system above Duskwater in Northern Ayrshire, near Dalry. Comments on the site warn that there is no easy or official access and that it is difficult to find. Spiritually, ALL caves are liminal places that are more than mere hollows in the rocks and have obvious roles in folklore. If there *is* such a thing as DNA Memory, then we must all get something of a frisson from these, that hearkens back to humanity's earliest dawn when caves were our first places of refuge and – often - worship.

In that respect I did get obsessed with a very similar cave a few years ago, and this one in West Wales once contained the remains of what became known as the *Red Lady of Paviland.* From the grave goods placed around the red-ochred bones, this seems to have been a shamanic figure dating back 30,000 years or more. In the event DNA testing confirmed that this should actually have been the Red **Lad** of Paviland, though not before some people seemed to make inner contacts with a Neolithic priestess figure. Although inaccessible to me these days because of advancing years and advancing tides, I spent many idle hours visualising that particular crack and trying to enter it. Did I succeed? Well, you might get my book and find out. The true revelation to me personally was my conviction that this Red Lad reincarnated in my era as Stan Gooch, a 'continuation' whose visionary books on Neanderthals were largely scorned by the establishment, yet have proved unerringly correct decades later. Despite a series of best-sellers, he died alone in extreme poverty in a caravan a mere bicycle ride or a stiff walk away from Paviland.

Stan Stan Stan… Under the Moon above my garden, in the light of tonight's promised view of the Aurora, I'll say your name.

Are all such entrances to Elphame in other parts of the country likely to contain the sort of teeny-tiny energies/entities described by Bessie Dunlop's peers? What about that evocative poem by 'Fiona McCleod', who excited the passions of the lovelorn W.B. Yeats before he found out this was a fella named William Sharp.

> *How beautiful they are, the lordly ones*
> *Who dwell in the hills, in the hollow hills.*
> *They have faces like flow'rs*
> *And their breath is a wind*
> *That blows over summer meadows*
> *Filled with dewy clover.*
> *Their limbs are more white than shafts of moonshine,*

They are more fleet than the March wind,
They laugh and are glad and are terrible
When their lances shake and glitter
Ev'ry green reed quivers.
How beautiful they are,
How beautiful,
The lordly ones in the hollow hills.

I suppose it's these Lordly Ones that attract me, rather than the cartoony miniatures described earlier. Years ago, when I was a teen, I worked through the visualisations given by the real magus Kim Seymour in his essays about the High Place of the Moon, that were full of this kind of faery.[4] When I saw Peter Jackson's 'Lord of the Rings' trilogy his elves were exactly as I always imagined and wanted. But at the moment, my glide and slide into Elphame doesn't seem to be taking me into that particular realm.

If interested, you should try to enter that Elphame Gateway using a good photograph and/or via your 'creative imagination' that Dr. Jung wrote about. Or indeed 'enter' any cave from your locality that might have myths attached. Build up the image and imagine yourself stepping into it. Be aware of the liminality; summon up an ambience. Write down what you saw or felt. Even if it is nothing. Try it on a regular basis, tying it in, perhaps, with the phases of the Moon. It is the simplest of magickal exercises. Don't be dismayed if nothing seems to happen. It is the directed effort that matters. Work work work... When you reach toward the Inners, 'They' reach toward you, often without you knowing (because They *are* you). Work that I did years ago, apparently without result at the time, eventually manifested itself unexpectedly and appropriately with great effect. 'They' don't seem to think of Time in the way we do. Even 'Lloyd' knew that: a day in his world was a year in ours.

There's a separate part toward the end of our garden that we feel is for our own 'Gentry'. I haven't 'seen' them but there were moments years ago when things inexplicably disappeared. So we acted 'as if', and also created a corner where we hung old wrist watches from a tall shrub, to

4   See T*he Inner Realms of Christine Hartley.*

create an area where Time Stops. We have also mounted on the garden arch what I really believe to be a Faery Bell. It's only about 3 inches tall, and this came from the doorway of gardener's cottage I lived in many years ago, in the enchanted valley of Murhill. I wrote all about these in my novel *The Moonchild,* which was an accurate depiction of that place. So whenever I enter this area I ring the bell thrice, asking for permission. I'm reminded of that Kevin Costner film 'Field of Dreams' with the tag-line *If you build it They will come...*

Oh I'm babbling here. I blame the heat. Forgive me.

My point being…

This afternoon, still on my quest for Elphame, I placed a deck-chair, in the shade, toward the end of our long and narrow garden, facing back toward our house. This was just before the section we dedicated to the Gentry. This area also contains the old blue shed, white roses, a blackberry bush, a few strawberries, a wheelbarrow, a small but vigorous Lilac Tree and various scattered tools when I forget to put them away of an evening. It used to contain my mountain bike, but I hated it and it hated me so I gave it away. Anyway, the chair was within reach of the small (12 inch) standing stone that seemed to call me on Solsbury Hill[5] near Bath. We sited this next to our frogless frog pond after putting some real gold for any interested Trows under its base. We always visualise them in passing, working away below the ground. They have given us *true* gold over the years.

So then I rang the bell and asked Them – whatever They are and in whatever form – for guidance and learning, and settled down into the chair to visualise this Ayrshire gateway to Elphame.

Of course I'd like to write something portentous like: 'Nothing happened – Everything happened'. In the event I drifted off into a deep, deep *deep* non-dreaming sleep, woken only when M brought me a cuppa tea and I got WhatsApps from all my daughters for Fathers' Day.

---

5   See *Searching for Sulis.*

Today, it is raining, lightly and thinly. Silver angled lines against the old red brick of our garden wall. I've got my forehead against the cool glass of the narrow patio door. M has just come in from adjusting the hidden crystal 'grid' that she created in our garden for her own Work. I must ask her later if I've shared too much in writing that.

You're peeping and muttering, Alan she whispered, sneaking up behind me.

I don't actually talk to myself, but sometimes my head is so full of stuff – usually guilty memories of stupid things I've done – that I have mutterings - short intense bursts. If they'd been swear words in public I'd apologise and explain/lie that I had Tourette's Syndrome and was seeking appropriate help, - via a hypnotist. As it is, this only happens in our house when I'm alone with my thoughts. My Dad used to come out with whole sentences in the quiet of the sitting room in Ashington when watching the telly – usually a co'boy - but then again he was having inner gunfights within the joyless marriage caused by his difficult wife (Mam) and useless son (Me).

Did you know, I said brightly to M, *That's what they used to say about Wizards?*

She didn't.

I didn't either, to be honest. It was just one of the phrases that Walter Ernest Butler mentioned somewhere – though not on the Town Bridge the other day. Well, I say 'the other day', but it could have been last week or even a month ago. Time is doing odd things. David Icke said Time is actually speeding up because of cosmic wars between alien races. But I think this is more to do with the simple process of ageing. The hours, days and forever-weeks dragged during my unhappy schooldays but are now mere blinks of the Time Goddess' eye today in my 70s. I think Icke's sense of 'speeding up' is less to do with the atmospheres of Elphame, or Giant Lizards masquerading as the Royal Family, and more because – like me – he's getting on a bit and is no longer the young Messiah in a turquoise jump-suit.

I had an idea. I decided to consult Neven – that is to say my big clunky phone. (I went to Tesco yesterday to see if I could trade it in for a smaller one, but the price quoted was ridiculous.) Still, Moto Neven, or M'Neven has a small button on the side that you can press and ask direct questions. To impress Margaret and prove to myself what a useless device my phone was I asked:

Tell me about Wizards that Peep and Mutter…

And almost instantly it came up with **Isaiah 8:19.** I don't need to look. To me the Old Testament is the Book of Many Evils. I also did it the slow way and Googled. Moto Neven with her android-powered brain promptly informed me that 'peep' means 'an unearthly sound; to speak out of the ground.' I like that. While 'mutter' refers to 'incantations of the Babylonian and Egyptian rituals, magical words.' I like that even better.

Despite myself, I was impressed. So I used that little dedicated button on the side again:

Tell me about NicNeven…

Almost instantly I got the response: *Nick Nevern. British actor in East Enders, Screenwriter and Director.*

Not bad, I must admit.

That hat was yesterday. The hot heat is back. It's the day of the solstice. Most of Wiltshire was probably up half the night at Stonehenge or Avebury, which aren't far from us. Me, I'm in the garden office on my pc and somewhat lost in huge spaces in my mind, finding even more stuff about NicNeven. It's as though all the references in cyber space have formed a queue to nudge me:

'Nicniven, with hir nymphes in number anew [enough]… The king of phairie, and his court, with the elf queine…'

The poet Montgomerie described her riding on Halloween with the elf king and queen and their court, so NicNeven is not necessarily seen by everyone as the Queen of Elphame, but a supporter. Yet the name of 'NicNevin' was *always* associated with Faery.

And then I read: 'A woman from Quarff on Shetland claimed to be acquainted with some local trows among whom was one Sara Neven.'

Trows trows trows!

I've often wondered why I'm in Trowbridge. For years, if you lived in the posher places of Bradford on Avon or Bath (as I did), Trowbridge was the only place where you could afford housing if your marriage broke up (as mine did). Even before Covid destroyed everything, and when it was still relatively thriving, it had a reputation (undeserved!) among the snobs for being a town of yobs: Trowbridge Trouts and Trowbridge Trolls, Karens and Chavs – or whatever the current insults are now. Such terms are ever-becoming, sneers without end when *snobbisme* forms its own nasty Wild Hunt.

None of the authorities had any agreement as to the origin of the name, and one pathetic authority suggested, without evidence, that it was from Tree Bridge, but I'm not having that. Apparently 'trow' is also an old word for 'to believe, to trust, or to think'.

The phrase 'If you believe in me, I'll believe in you', just floated in. *Alice in Wonderland?* I suppose I can fit that together with 'If you build it They will come.'

Well, in the light of everything I've learned over the 23 years I've lived here, very happily, I am going to say that for me, I will *believe* and *trust* that Trow means *trow*, another word for troll.

I'm not sure how these critturs got down here in Southern England, as they were first spoken about in the Orkney and Shetland Islands and seem to have come from Norway in any case.

'The archetypal trow was an ugly, mischievous, little creature that resided in the ancient mounds scattered across Orkney… Although some tales declared that a trow could pass for a human - although usually old, wizened or deformed - in general they were said to be short, ugly, stunted creatures and considerably smaller than a man.'[6]

I'm sure the trolls spoke very highly of the human observers too. But their descriptions in folklore exactly match that of the Faeries:

> Within their earthen mounds - known locally as howes or knowes - the dwelling-places of the trows were said to be sumptuous and dazzling. Gold, silver and previous materials were said to decorate the walls, while only fine food and drink was served at their tables. Deep inside these magical halls, the trows would satisfy their insatiable passion for music and dancing, very often luring mortal fiddlers inside to perform at their otherworldly celebrations.

---

6   http://orkneyjar.com/folklore/trows/

And somehow I find myself considering NicNeven again. She keeps buzzing around my mind like the fly that has just buzzed into the coolth of our sitting room. I can't blame it for that, given the scorching world beyond. In the olden days I would have whacked it with a tightly rolled-up newspaper; now I must go *Hmmm...*

Is that you, Neven? Or your pal Queen Mab? Apparently the latter easily assumed such forms without losing any power. I managed to get the fly out into the garden and maybe Mab as well.

I've also learned that Nicnevin was also sometimes known as the fearsome 'gyre-carlin', this being the Lowland equivalent of the *cailleach*, or hag, a well-armed, violent and partially cannibalistic being. I suppose you'd call her a man-eater – or does that phrase date and damn me?

On the other hand – and this important - this particular faery was also linked to cloth-making. It used to be said that, if unspun flax was not removed from the distaff at the end of the year, the gyre-carling *aka* NicNeven would steal it all. Conversely, if a woman asked for help in spinning, this particular faery would enable the supplicant to do three to four times as much work as other spinners.

I wouldn't want to cross you Neven...

But I can't help noticing that Trowbridge was once made wealthy by the cloth-making industry, and the dear River Biss was a potent source of power for the various engines needed. Trowbridge's scale of production was such it was described as the 'Manchester of the West'. It had over 20 woollen cloth producing factories, making it comparable to northern industrial towns.

If I tried to find out how an apparently Shetland or Orcadian name came to be embedded here in my town, I'd find myself being spun and twisted like that rock art I tried but failed to find in the Simonside Hills of the Borderlands when my life was similarly being spun and twisted – and I dare say that most of the people reading this will have known similar.

I don't think I can ever make actual human *sense* of Faery. Much as I love Scotland, I don't want to go up there physically – at least not until I've had all the ops I need to get my bits and pieces sorted after the heart attack. Some things just are, and you have to go with them, no matter how insensible.

NicNeven, NicNeven, NicNeven… Queen of Elphame?

I'm actually wondering if I met her in the Atrium last week. Or was it last month? Or maybe, with Time doing its twisty swirly things like the carved rock patterns at Roughting Linn in Northumberland, it happened in the future? Not as any kind of spirit manifestation (at least I don't think so) but as a Continuation. Although in my fantasies I'd like her to appear in the style of Cate Blanchett as Galadriel in *Lord of the Rings*, in the folklore of 'true' stories she first appears incognito. Usually down at heel. Somewhat dumpy. Easily ignored or scorned. Quickly forgotten. That's how she first appeared to Andro and Marion and Bessie and a host of others.

For me, it happened like this…

I was sitting near the cosmic Vending Machine and scribbling a reply to the Welsh *bon-viveur* who uses the name David Conway. He'd been unwell, which was unusual for him. So I wrote back telling him that I'd created a personalised healing talisman, using sigils and energies from the Abra-Melin system and had just posted it First Class (all letters on magickal stuff *have* to be First Class). On receipt of such a thing from a mighty mage like *moi*, he would soon be well and as envious of my good looks as ever. Of course, it is simply a ScratchCard with a top prize of £500,000. Knowing him, he is bound to win it. Knowing him, he will deny it ever arrived. That was last week. Or was it last month? Or have I yet to send it?

[*In the Halls of Maat, I imagine that our Bodies of Light will appear as something akin to the above.*]

Anyway, back to my possible encounter with *a* Queen of Elphame, or at least a Continuation…

As I scribbled my Timeless Prose to the Master I was half aware of a dumpy, poorly-dressed, rough-looking woman 'of a certain age', getting or giving grief of some kind to a woman from the Council, who had a red clip-board, a bunch of forms and a very wearied expression. With my hearing (or lack of) I couldn't/needn't make out what was going on and the communication between them was bursts of sounds like you might get if you removed all the consonants from words. I got up and was about to go when I saw the woman give the unmistakable sign of *Thank You.*

As I've written before, 'British Sign Language' is my second language, the learning of which has been the best thing I've ever done. Across the length of the room I got the woman's attention and the conversation went along the lines of:

Deaf you? Hearing Impaired me. Signing learn me. Before before before.

The council worker made excuses and left. The woman's face was radiant. But no sooner had we started signing than a fella joined us, a poorly dressed *really* rough-looking chap of about the same age who had been sitting alone on the other side of the room. He had seen our exchange and it turned out he was also profoundly deaf and a signer.

Name you what? Is the first phrase everyone learns in BSL.

They told me.

Name me... I finger-spelled **Al**, for brevity.

Deaf signers are very rare in this area. The two people were unconnected. Their faces shone and so did mine. I felt like a match-maker. I was also startled when they finger-spelled their names, but thought nothing of it at the time. I won't tell you these because **a)** it might be indiscreet **b)** you wouldn't believe me.

I can only say that, in the realms of faery that are obsessing me, they were *entirely* appropriate.

I then turned my head away for second but when I turned back they were gone.

No, No, thrice No – that DIDN'T happen! Although it would have made a cracking yarn if it had. I don't want to do a Castaneda or a Hubbard on people.

Quite simply we parted amiably with the signs: *Happy man me. See you again. Future future.* Then like Elvis I left the building without a backward glance or speculative thought.

I hope the pair are still together and happy, their faces shining like faeries are supposed to shine because of the white/light blood that makes them different from us. Maybe they're in what *we* might see as a rundown house in rough council estate, but which in *their* eyes is an elfin palace fit for the noblest of trows. And maybe they're musing on the strange being and Weaver of Fates who brought them together.

In their eyes, who or what was *I* a Continuation of?

I hope I'm not boring any of my readers still with me. I hope you don't think this book is entirely self-indulgent. What I'm hoping – actually, what I'm *predicting* – is that some time after reading this you will find yourself on a bridge in your own town. It doesn't matter what country this might be. This doesn't have to be an ancient rustic, stone bridge in a pretty location flanked by those hawthorn trees favoured by faery; it could be like that powerful truck-bearing steel structure I stood on overlooking the Monongahela River in Morgantown; it could be just a few planks over a stream in some unmemorable field; or something bland and hardly noticeable like this one over the Biss that I'm writing about. But – and I promise you this will happen – for a micro-second you will think of my crossings over the Biss and everything in my head will be in yours… the currents, the swirls, the atmospheres the Continuations. And the word 'Elphame' will pop into your mind and you will go *Hmmmm….* And realise that you're part of all this and always were, but with your own routes to choose on the other side.

I've spent the morning walking into town early before The Scorching begins, and get my 10K steps done without melting onto the pavements. I saw a film with Vin Diesel in which he played Riddick, the 'Last of the Furyans', a very angry, tough elf-like being who is stranded on an alien planet where he has to escape from regular immolations. (I feel the elven clans themselves would enjoy watching this with me.) It's a bit like that in Trowbridge this morning, although no-one is ever likely to confuse me with Vin Diesel, whose real name is the rather prosaic Mark Sinclair

I've learned that the fae are particularly fond of hawthorn trees and I'd shelter under one if I could find any. Trowbridge does have a large and excellent park but I'm not sure if any of the quite majestic trees are 'Thorns. So first, I have to Google to see what they look like...

I know, I know, I know… I must seem surprisingly and exasperatingly ignorant. In fact, my Mam in a rage once described Dad as 'the most ignorantest man she'd ivver knaan', and I've inherited something of this. (On the other hand, when it comes to aircraft recognition from 1937 up until 1970 I have no peers).

So where is NicNeven today? Has she/It/They appeared yet?

*Niss*Neven *Niss*Neven *Niss*Neven I peep and mutter under my breath, pausing only to send good wishes upstream to the Source. I've also learned, through googling on my phone during a sleepless night (not to be recommended!) that there are alternative derivations of this name, such as *NicNaomhin*, 'Daughter of the Little Saint' and *NicCreamhain*, 'Daughter of the little Tree Man.' How can I not like that last one? I *must* find myself a Hawthorn tree. I'll ask M when I get home, as she's bound to know where to find one.

However, musings apart, I was quite surprised to see a young woman to my left clutching what seems to be sheaves of wheat, seemingly unfazed by the sun.

Do I know you?

You didn't come to see me, Alan.

A fat memory buzzes and flits like that fly and lands on my brow. I leave it.

Cornwall. Too far. I was broke. With a baby. You're Ithell aren't you. Ithell Colquhoun.

You didn't come.

Your friend said you had dementia.

Why are you calling me now?

Am I? Is trying to remember something you once wrote the same as calling you?

It is to me.

Ithell, it was something about the – and these are your words – the forces within the land, the praeternatural contacts that have been lost.

Rather good. Thank you.

I thought it was. And there was a long paragraph in your book 'Living Stones' about rock strata and its effects. That was what I was experiencing down Murhill. I know you saw the cosmos as interdepedent and interconnected, even the minutiae effecting everything and everyone else.

> *Find the book. Use it. Pretend that you're hearing it from me. In a sense you are.*
>
> *Cut and paste?*
>
> *Paste. The cutting and saving into your spirit was done when you first read it. The words never quite left your mind.*
>
> *Limpley Stoke and Murhill were for me in those years, what Lamorna in Cornwall was for you.*
>
> *I had Dion Fortune in my mind then. For years and years.*
>
> *We all did.*

I've still got your marvellous book 'The Sword of Wisdom'. Battered copies on E-Bay are selling for £150.00. I do wish I'd met you.

She frowned, faded and shimmered a bit. I spoke hurriedly before I lost her:

*Maybe in a parallel timeline where I made different choices I **did** get to meet you.*

Then we must keep on nodding terms with all of ourselves.

And with the parallel Fae, whom you saw all the time in Lamorna?

Especially the Fae.

So now I scan, I cut, I paste, while trying (though not desperately) to remember the name of Ithell's friend who had made her way down to Murhill after reading my book 'Gate of Moon'. It was double-barrelled. She seemed to have a grace-and-favour apartment somewhere very posh in London. *Pat Pat Pat...?* She made a sort of mini-pilgrimage to find me as she thought I might have been a Master of Magic. So did I. We've both been disappointed in that respect.

Anyway, here is what Ithell 'said' to me in her own way:

> The life of a region depends ultimately on its geologic substratum, for this sets up a chain reaction which passes, determining their character, in turn through its streams and wells, its vegetation and the animal life that feeds on this,

and finally through the type of human attracted to live there. In a profound sense also the structure of its rocks gives rise to the psychic life of the land: granite, serpentine, slate, sandstone, limestone, chalk and the rest each have their special personality, dependent on their age in which they were laid down, each being co-existent with a special phase of the earth-spirit's manifestation.[7]

NicNeven NicNeven NicNeven – if you call her she will come. Although I'm inclined to believe that if you do call, it's because she's already here. Somehow. Somewhere. Someway.

In Judika Illes *Encyclopedia of Spirits*, I learn that NicNevin can transform water into rocks and sea into dry land but I wouldn't ask her to do anything like that. According to Ms. Illes 'Her' name is from the Gaelic *Nic an Neamhain*, meaning 'Daughter of Frenzy'. She flies through the night, invisibly, along with or even leading the Wild Hunt. The Romans, sticking their noses in, somehow identified her with Diana. When Scotland officially converted to Christianity this former Goddess was was reclassified as both a Faery and a Demon.

What's not to like about that?

NicNevin, NicNevin, NicNevin...

My new 'pash NicNevin also seems to be identical with that spirit with the odd and perhaps ugly name *Gyre-Carlin*. Sir Walter Scott (author of the now-unreadable 'Ivanhoe'), also did sterling work on Scottish faeries but the wee scunner called my erstwhile Lady a hag! a 'gigantic and malignant female' who rides on storms. More likely she *was* the spirit of the storm itself, Walter - don't be nasty. Of course he also linked her to witches, who became the scapegoats for everything in those days. A witch from Crieff tried in

---

7   *The Living Stones*, 2016. Also see John Kruse' *The Spirits of the Land*

about 1615 was called Catherine Nevin, reinforcing this association, and it was thought that she got her surname from her neighbours because they identified her with the faery queen. The same may well be the case for another 'witch' and folk healer, Margaret NicLevine of Bute, who was tried in 1662.

I've never liked my name 'Alan Richardson'. When I first started writing, aged 17, I thought about using a pen-name like Basil Wilby did with his moniker 'Gareth Knight', but couldn't think of anything apt. Maybe it's not too late to adopt the name Nevin? Alan Nevin? It's a masculine name of Irish origin, meaning 'Little Bone' or 'Little Saint'. Maybe I'll form a secret group called 'Clan Nevin', like Robert Cochrane's wiccan 'Clan of Tubal Cain'. Not that there was anything ancient about Cochrane's coven; he just lifted the name from Graves' 'The White Goddess'. Nothing wrong with that. I'm always lifting stuff from everyone. For Northumbrians, during the days of the cross-Border Reivers, this was once a way of life. I used to steal small things from shops when I was a boy. That must be in my DNA too[8].

Yet for some reason or non-reason or perhaps inner plane or web-enchantment the name 'Gyre-Carling' keeps popping up and is somehow, according to some commentators, also associated with **Hecate**, the goddess of boundaries, transitions, crossroads, magic, the New Moon, necromancy, and ghosts, though I'm not quite sure how they connect. Haven't had a chance to dive into this arcanum yet but I'll have to do so eventually as Hecate 'bothered' me many years ago. And still does. And if you carry on reading, before too long we will both get bothered.

Today is the hottest heat I've ever known in this country. It was 44C in our back yard. I've been told that the faeries don't like the Sun much and are Moon and Star beings. M is all togged up ready to go to the Rock Choir in nearby Westbury. The outfit is a fetching witch-black with a gurt big star over the heart. As I watch, I'll be wondering if there's an inner-plane 'Clan Nevin' taking everything in, on all levels. I do feel that there's a spare place in the back of my mind that will be

---

8   To my daughters and grandchildren...this was WRONG.

spinning and knitting all these thoughts and things and connections together, just as M in her spare moments is busy knitting something for our youngest grandchild.

Westbury… I've written about Westbury before, somewhere[9]. It has a huge White Horse carved onto the overlooking hillside. The hillside is at the northernmost edge of the Salisbury Plain. The Salisbury Plain is a great wodge of land covering large parts of Wiltshire. Wiltshire is home to Stonehenge, Avebury and a host of other little known or largely-ignored ancient sites. They have recently reintroduced formerly extinct Bustards to breed, grow and run free, safe from the public. The tankies and gunners have strict orders to leave them alone. The public, of course, can't get near them, so they will forever be safe among the long barrows. One of them contained the bones of a Queen, with the long skull that hints at all sorts of evolutions and mysteries.

I suppose that if I keep writing about these places in tome after tome, it's because I've stayed in the same place for year after year. And the Spirits of these Places, as I keep insisting, have their own tales to tell and want to be heard. Or am I making excuses for being repetitive?

I blab. Or do I mean *WE* blab? – me and the Places that is. I'm a long way from the Northern England and geo-historical Borders of the NicNeven and Elphame, but it's all within me. I am in the south west and also the north east, but in a different time stream.

But Westbury, as I was saying… I was very proud to see M in her all-black Rock Choir outfit with the big star over her heart centre. The choir does various gigs in the locality, for various charitable organisations

---

9   *Visions of Paviland,* I think.

such as the Alzheimers Society; membership is totally inclusive, all are welcome, regardless.

They lined up under the great tree next to Westbury Library

NicNevin NicNevin NicNevin I invoked in an undertone, 'peeping and muttering', saying the name but with lips closed. Anyone next to me might have thought I was just humming, rather than trying to summon/awaken/encourage an ancient Witch Queen whose true home was in Elphame.

And then the choir began. I hadn't a clue as to the song or the singer, but the words rather startled me:

> *Life is a mystery*
> *Everyone must stand alone*
> *I hear you call my name*
> *And it feels like home*
>
> *When you call my name, it's like a little prayer*
> *I'm down on my knees, I wanna take you there*
> *In the midnight hour, I can feel your power*
> *Just like a prayer, you know I'll take you there*

Good grief, is that you Nevin?! Yes, I AM calling you! I suppose it IS a little prayer. And yes, until M arrived I'd been standing alone in this odd realm all my life. Yes, you CAN come in the night!

You can see that the words were entirely appropriate to my invocation.

Yes Yes Yes, I **now** know (coz M told me) that this was *Like a Prayer* by Madonna, but I lost interest in musick when Cat Stevens retired; I wouldn't know Madonna from the Lady Babalon – if indeed they're not the same being.

Other things happened at that meet, but I have a horror of becoming a bore. It did seem to me that Nevin, or her group consciousness, made herself manifest to me that day via all sorts of interwoven events, right there on the melting high street of Westbury during their annual fete, and I met the man I hope to become when I grow up.

Long story. Enough said.

Thank you, Thank you, Thank you…

At last it's grey today, cool and perfect. I'm in the Atrium of the Wiltshire Council again, wearing jeans and jacket and not those embarrassing shorts that make me feel like an overgrown schoolboy. It strikes me that perhaps I can squeeze in some parallel or analogue here, with my notions of Group Minds and inner-plane Clans? Or bees in hives? The Council pays my pension, so I'm interwoven with people here in all sorts of ways.

The 'University of the Third Age' is gathering so it must be Tuesday. M is with her sister at Corsham, visiting a Knitting Adeptus to try to understand where they're going wrong with the pattern they have for our respective grandchildren. When they started, they aimed for the boys' first birthday; now they are nearly two, twice the size, and their sweaters so far are still without arms.

I actually know some of this U3A group. I worked with them in the Library Service, when its HQ was based directly opposite here in Chapman's Building, on the banks of the Biss. And also, a couple who knew me from where I worked before that, as an Instructor for Adults with Learning Disabilities and Special Needs at the Ashton Street Centre, also in Trowbridge. Both buildings were razed for the Council's own special needs of a budgetary nature, though they claimed it was to do with 'modernisation' of the service. Well they *would* say that wouldn't they? No-one believed them. A few of the U3A lot see me writing. They've always liked me and known me to be harmless, despite my books being so weird. They come over. Anticipating this I've prepared a special page on my jotter.

'This one is all about *you* [N and N],' I say archly, and read out a fake, slightly suggestive piece about them being secret Orgy-Masters and Mistresses of Brokerswood. 'This is just the first Volume of what I'm gonna reveal.' I promise each one at least a chapter, telling All. They glow. I can see the story-lines flashing in their auras, just like the 'Elphame' broadsheet flashed in mine. The Wild Hunt's new leader calls them back to normality and they snort and gallop out, goodness knows where, coz, there really isn't anything sylvan in this part of town at all, though probably a lot of dead souls that need rescuing.

What has just floated into my thoughts is a memory of what I must call my 'Vision of the Weavers'. I suppose this yarn is appropriate now as the notion of weaving comes up again and again with respect to Nic Nevin and the Gyre-Carling. There are numerous Weaving Goddesses, though no Weaving Gods that I can find, but I don't suppose we need to agonise about gender in this Aeon. I'll just give a brief mention of the main names:

- **Arianrhod** was the Celtic Goddess of fertility, rebirth and the weaving of cosmic Time and Fate, whose name means silver-wheel, the ever-turning wheel of the year.
- **Athena/Minerva** the goddesses of weaving from the Greek and Roman Mystery Traditions.
- **Neith** the Egyptian goddess of creation, wisdom, weaving, and war. (I quite like her.)
- **Frigg** is the wife of Odin and the Norse goddess of spinning and weaving. She is said to have woven the clouds, mists, and fog, and gives her name to (in my memory) pleasant sexual activities also.

But there are also **The Moirai**, or the Three Fates, and these three sisters work together. Like the witches and faeries of Elphame, as described by the Christian persecutors, they were described as lame, ugly old women. They were:

Klotho who spins the thread of human life.
Lakhesis who then draws it out.
Atropos who does the final cut.

Klotho was the primary figure. Does her name have any connection with the word 'cloth'? She not only chose who was born, but also decided when gods or mortals were to be saved or put to death. You might think she was a nasty piece of work to be avoided at all costs but I'm not sure if we have much choice.

These Beings/Energies/Currents/Flows/Entwinements must effect us all, Human and – as far I understand this – Faery also.

I do believe that I met the three of them in 1985 in Bennington Street, Cheltenham...

Before I yarn, I must apologise in case I'm doing the thing that Old Men do... repeat stories that everyone has heard a dozen times, improving upon them with each re-telling. Though, thinking upon that, I suppose that this too is an act of weaving as I attempt to spin a good *yarn*[10].

I was visiting the crusty old magus William G. Gray with a view to  doing his biography. Far more important than that, I was still buzzing because of the appearance in my life of my first daughter, Zoë. Bill didn't like children; he didn't like many adults either. He was positively scathing about the dismal life anyone from this generation would experience. 38 years later I would have a right go at him about this in my book 'Scattering Light – the Quantum Entanglement of William G. Gray and Alan Richardson', but then I just kept quiet.

_____

10 I didn't see that coming. I think that's rather clever!

'You won't have any more,' he said, in that detached way way he had when he energised his (formidable) clairvoyance, for which I had a very healthy respect.

I felt chilled. My wife had been told by a doctor only that morning that her womb had been tilted after Zoë's birth, and she may not be able to have more children.

Well… what happened next was both instant and timeless. I seemed to zoom 'upward' and found myself in a rustic room with a high ceiling and wooden rafters and a floor covered with what I thought was weaving machines – wheels and spindles and all the other pieces of kit I know nothing about – and three women operating them.

I'm not sure how, but I communed with these hitherto unknown and un-named until now 'Weavers of Fate'.

No No NO! The future that Gray saw will NOT be mine. Weave differently.

That's as best as I can describe my single, angry outburst before I 'descended' again and found myself staring dumbly and numbly at Bill.

So, if you've followed my writing before this book, you will know that my three other daughters appeared in due course and proved Bill's magery to be fallible.

My point being, it is always worth challenging the Moirai if you think they're weaving for you something dreadful. With the usual caveat of 'Be careful what you wish for…'

M is at home practising for another Rock Choir this afternoon at Frome: a subtly 'alternative' town that has always seemed to speak to me on subtle and alternative levels. Me, I'm scribbling this on my much-battered notebook in the completely empty and somewhat echoey Atrium. It being a Saturday, all the Council workers are at home, leaving only the adjoining Library open.

Am a bit melancholic at the moment, but that's not necessarily a bad thing. Sometimes my melancholy can be oddly tasty, like sucking on a sweet-and-sour lolly. But I'm not sure if my *Journey toward Elphame* is taking you - the reader – anywhere. I'd hoped that the whole process would work by a sympathetic vibration, if that's the right term. A musick teacher at my old school once tapped a large tuning fork to set it thrumming like an angry bee and then put it near (but not touching) other tuning forks, and they started thrumming also.

I might have made that up. But you get the idea.

Hello Violet, I say, as a very young version of Violet Firth appears to the side of me. There's no-one else in the Atrium; she could have manifested to full physical appearance and gone through the whole Invoking Ritual of the Pentagram chanting the Words of Power and no-one would have noticed.

> *I'm exasperated, Alan.*
> *I don't blame you. We're both thrumming like tuning forks.*

In my case it's because various young folk keeping posting a ridiculous photograph of 'Dion Fortune' on Facebook. I keep saying It's NOT her but they won't let up. The photograph is used on an otherwise accurate and detailed Wikipedia entry. I wouldn't mind if it even looked vaguely like 'Dion Fortune' but it seems to me insultingly absurd. Yet dozens on Facebook and gawd-knows how many other sites are taking this for granted and using it to make their own inner connections. The photo

keeps appearing and landing on my various screens, like the big fat stupid fly that was bothering me. I want to swat it. Am I being unnecessarily crabby here? If anyone used a photo of, say, a young Brad Pitt to represent me, would I whinge?

I'm sure there's a lesson or a moral in this, given what I've already said about the mind's need to create shapes and forms with respect to the Fae.

> *It is **not** me, Alan...*

And so she goes.

(The inane picture continues to annoy me. For some reason the name 'Mabel Dodge Luhan' floated into my mind when I first saw this. You might want to Google her, but it will take you deep into D.H. Lawrence and Taos and New Mexico and Plumed Serpent realms that are far far from the coolth of Elphame.)

I crossed the Biss several times today but didn't notice. I'm also a bit frightened. It's been nearly a year since my spectacular heart attack and helicopter flight, and while I feel I'm slowly getting stronger physically there's a part of myself that is scouring all the personas I've used and misused over nearly 7 decades – usually at the expense of others. I'll be better, I'm sure, when I've got a date for the removal of the bladder/Mab stone. And even better when it's actually done.

This might just be an Age Thing when I wonder if every book I write might be my Last. I've been saying this for 40 years now but I fear that when I've finished this attempt to slip-slide into Elphame, that **They** will see it as job done for this life and call me over.

My Dad once promised via a brilliant medium that he would appear when it's my time and take me across. Mind you, as he never went further than Newcastle on the local bus, I'm not sure he'll be the best guide for entering the Infinite — whatever it might be like. I'm determined to outlive him though. He died from a heart attack at 77, so that means I've got at the very leastest 5 happy years left.

When M reads this she will wag her finger like a wand; she will wag it so fiercely that you'll see sparks and will tell me that she wants a LOT more years than that. I'm sure she'll get them.

This morning I strolled to one of my local tea shoppes and got there just after opening. This one is Leykers, and I've only just realised – honest – that its address is in White Hart Yard – deeply powerful symbolism in that, methinks! The White Hart symbolises the existence of the Otherworld and also indicates that forces from the Otherworld are present and already in action.

So I ordered my usual and then go to the Upper Room. There are often three others already deep into their own rituals of newspapers, coffee, i-Phone or books. Being British, we don't acknowledge each other; our unconnected group with disparate lives sits like Quakers in their silent services. (If you ever come here when I'm there, please don't interrupt us.)

In my troubled youth, I would have smoked and stared into space and tried to become like Shiva and destroy my world and its miseries. These days I sit in a corner and open whatever book I carry about with me for such moments and let things float through me, Biss-like.

In this case I kept thinking about the slim white tree in our long and narrow garden. If it's a nice day I sit in our 'gravity chair' within the invisible 'grid' that M has created and muse over the tree's lines. I remember when we bought it as a shrub from a garden centre in Bath, and it only just squeezed into the back of our Suzuki Jimny. Now, maybe 5 years later (though it feels like 5 weeks and sometimes only 5 days) it's about 20 feet high and curves slightly from right to left, like a bow. I don't remember what sort of tree it is but will ask M who magicks everything.

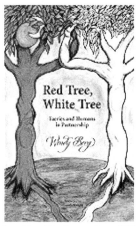

I mention the tree because the book I'm re-re-reading here in the Upper Room at White Hart Yard, is Wendy Berg's 'Red Tree, White Tree – Faeries and Humans in Partnership'. If I'm ever asked to name one book on magick I wish *I'd* written, it would be this. It is luminously silver-light Fae years ahead and beyond anything else I've read. I envy Wendy her knowledge and the experiences that helped create this.

However I'm not *totally* following those paths into Faeryland and trying to access Elphame by a side route. It makes something of a heretic, I suppose, but I'm not a devotee of the Grail Mysteries. I'll try not to mount my high white hobby-horse here, but in brief it seems to me that the Grail Mysteries have almost become an Orthodoxy within the Western Mystery Tradition, along with that 'mighty all-embracing glyph' of the Kabbalistic 'Tree of Life'. People have made comfortable livings writing about them and offering weekend residential courses and on-line or even personalised graded teachings. I might simply be jealous here, so take that into account. I've known, or known *of*, several people who have had powerful Grail Visions and then devoted their lives to this Quest. I can't say that in human terms they manifested any greater Grace than the rest of us. They didn't shine with inward light or pulsate with love or say anything jaw-droppingly wise or demonstrate any neo-shamanic talents beyond Path Workings. William G. Gray's explosive, life-changing Grail Vision that led him to form the Sangreal Sodality brought him nothing but disappointment, misery, a sense of betrayal from all his supposed followers at every level and ended with a death as painful and desperate as Andro Man's[11] but far more prolonged.

So 'my' Elphame, as far as I'm understanding it, is somewhat removed from the Arthurian Mysteries. I'm not sure that NicNevin and Guinevere would get along, or even been on the same level of perception. I'm hoping that if I ever do glimpse Elphame that it will be a Grail-free Zone.

Hmmm...

As I muse again upon our singular White Tree (worryingly cracked along its slim trunk after recent gales) I can't help but create in my mind's eye a Red Tree on the *other* side of our narrow garden to mirror and complete the arch. Or rather, if I had skill I'd draw an elegant glyph to show both trees having roots that curve underground and meet, forming a circle.

Here's a glyph I tried to make. The tree on the left should be red.

This pops into my mind a lot.

A Star Gate? Lovely concept that! I'll visualise myself going through this and will tell you where it might lead – if anywhere. The effort alone is important. Sending out signals. Try it yourself and let me know, I'd love to hear. Just don't interrupt me if I'm having tea in some café.

---

11   See my *Scattering Light* about this.

I realise that in the broadest sense 'Elphame' is always on the edge of my (i.e. your/our) everyday doings. I suppose it's a bit like the 'Cloud' connected with computer networks.

I had my weekly coven meet this afternoon: nine good men and true, plus three powerful and delightful Crones. I use that word as an honorific, and so would you if you saw them. Even before the young Magister appears carrying the Book we all quietly circle the large hall, widdershins, in silence.

Nevin Nevin Nevin I peep and mutter at every step, inviting her in at the side of my mind.

As you will have guessed this is my Cardiac Rehab Class, the Magister in this case being a strapping young lad called Andy whose Book contains all our names, emergency contacts, medication, blood pressures and records our pulse rates before, during and after the various intense physical exercises we do for each session.

I doubt if any any of us will meet socially, but I'm slowly getting fragments of information from some of them as the weeks pass. Three of the older-than-me men who introduced themselves have come from the same part of Scotland where Andro Man breathed his last within the pyre.

Maybe we are all a Continuation of his coven.

I can give you a magick word today. It is supposed to be untranslatable. I promise that it will create a frisson within you even if you *have* heard it before.

So... in the beginning was the Word, and the Word was **HIRAETH.**

Pronounced pronounced 'here-eyeth' with a roll of the 'r'.

It is Welsh of course and thus the language of the true Ancient Brits.

I understand its meaning exactly and have always known it, but if I can cut-and-paste from Wikipedia:

> A spiritual longing for a home which maybe never was. Nostalgia for ancient places to which we cannot return. It is the echo of lost places of our soul's past and out grief for them. It

is the wind and the rocks, and the waves. It is nowhere and it is everywhere.

I've been visualising that underworld/overworld White Tree/Red Tree glyph a lot. Sometimes I try to step through it but so far without anything happening. Usually the image breaks and I end up falling into dreamless sleep. If I travelled into Elphame in spirit I certainly haven't had any poignant dreams about it.

Of course I'm aware that if I ever did step boldly into Elphame for a few moments then I might suffer the fate of so many others: on their return they find that generations have passed in the mortal world and they were no more than a piece of folklore.

On the other hand a slight parallel constantly occurs when writing this. I dap into the garden office for a quick browse of the Web to get a few tiny but important details, and the next thing I know two hours have passed.

During one of these incursions I stumbled upon Tam the Rhymer – remember him? After following a milk-white hart he met the actual Queen of Elfland herself, who told him to put his head on her knee, and thence showed him three marvels: the road to Hell, the road to Heaven, and the road to her home of the Elves. She also gives him the gift of prophecy, as well as the inability to tell a lie.

Maybe one of the fellas in Leykers as it overlooks White Hart Yard was/is a Continuation? Who knows where they go when they finish their coffee.

He became known as 'True Thomas' because he cannot tell a lie. I don't think I'd like him. I've known two people - male, female and unconnected – who loudly stated that they cannot lie, and ALWAYS tell the truth. And so they did, and wondered why they had no friends. They were both self-serving, arrogant individuals who had to get their own way and didn't care if they hurt or even devastated other people's feelings through their 'truth-telling'. If I ever do stumble into Elphame and meet True Thomas I'll stumble right back out again.

He was a real historical character who seems to have died around 1294, and his prophecies seem to have been accurate.

But if you want to find about a truer seer than True Tom, then you might want to Google the 'Brahan Seer', known in his native Scottish Gaelic as Coinneach Odhar, or Dark Kenneth, *aka* Kenneth Mackenzie. He was, according to legend, a staggeringly accurate predictor of the future who lived in the 17th century. Some have questioned whether the Seer existed at all, but what do they know, eh?

If ever a soul was half faery he was.

Is.

Will be.

I've just had a busy night, inwardly, and made tenuous contact with my Ancestral background **and** caught a glimpse of a faery. I owe it all to a bollard in the Biss.

I saw the bollard yesterday, dumped in another part of the river I hadn't crossed. Its top was just cresting the surface and the fierce flow around it created a small whirlpool. I thought of Corryvrekan again. Remember how that idiotic oceanologist gave the cause of this swirling as being an upright bollard-like rock below the surface? Obviously, it was all down to the excellent Sea Witch of that area, but anyway…the notion and image of the spiral kept re-appearing in my thoughts.

Because I couldn't sleep I went into the spare room so as not to disturb M, whose birthday it was the previous day. While there, I got a message on the personal magick mirror of my clunky Tesco Moto phone. It told me that my membership of the Facebook page for Cavan in Ireland had been accepted, and if I wanted to track down my ancestors there I would be welcome. I scrolled down through the postings and saw dozens of lost souls trying to find their own forebears.

Hmmm… That can wait until tomorrow I thought, when I get on my big pc in the garden office and M is walking with her pal on Salisbury Plain and then lunching with daughter Jade.

The spiral again. And again. I kept thinking about it and also the 'Star Gate' I had tried to create. The spiral seemed to be within the Gate. I tried to swirl in and through to Elphame or some galaxy far far from here but my imagination stopped short as though it hit glass.

Hmmm…

(I do that a lot! It's more useful than *Om*, which I've always thought rather passé even if it is the undertone of the Universe.)

What if I did get through, but like a thousand folk before me I couldn't get back, like Robert Kirk at Aberfoyle who used to 'bother' me... I don't really want to disappear from this world. Like Bilbo Baggins there are still adventures I want to have.

But... what if this creation of White and Red Tree was not a Star 'Gate' but a Star *Window*? Or even a small Star *Mirror* that I could hold between my hands and use for scrying?

Because I had spent numerous hours actually drawing the original with a variety of pens and endless amounts of sweaty, sweary frustration, chucking aside numerous naff efforts before the less-naff final one, it remained solid within my imagination.

So I relaxed, held my thoughts gently, peered into the swirls and saw peering back a small, pure-white, ethereal elfin creature! Pure translucent flesh, very small, it wasn't clothed. A Pixie? The Irish and Scottish named pixies as the *Aos Sí* (also spelled *Aos Sidhe*), and they were believed to inhabit ancient underground sites such as stone circles, barrows, dolmens, ringforts, or menhirs. In traditional regional lore, pixies are generally benign, mischievous, short of stature, and childlike. The Cornish word 'Pisky' also floated into my mind. Not that long ago almost every household in Cornwall had some kind of Pisky charm to attract the luck that the good will of the Piskies was thought to bring. Although they were said to have a wicked sense of humour, they would help anyone who treated them with respect.

I'll treat you with respect I said, before I lost the contact through sheer surprise. *I want to learn*, I added, and the moment ended.

As if that were not enough, when the full light of morning arrived and I took M her morning coffee and she wondered at my bewildered expression, I got a posting from Facebook. It seems that today, July 7th 2023, is known as as *Elven Star Day* because the date resolves, numerologickally, into 777. This is a day they assure us, when a portal opens between Elven realms and Human. If I hadn't had that very real and strong contact I might have sneered (I used to be good at sneering when I was younger and omniscient) but something certainly opened for me in the pre-dawn light. Age has wearied my omniscience somewhat, and my years now certainly condemn.

If my sums are right, I suppose the next 777 day won't be until July 7th 2032.

A strange week. We went on holiday. I won't say exactly where. It was idyllic: picture postcard village, cafés, ancient pubs, cute little shops, stunning scenery, stylish apartment with startling views. Yet on the second day M and I both confessed that we felt oddly depressed. For no reason that we could explain. Our heart should have sang is this place had everything we both love and need. In terms of sheer beauty it ranked a clear 9 out of 10, whereas dear old Trowbridge could never climb to more than a 3. We did the usual – walks in stunning countryside, cafes, meals out – but we left a day early and didn't feel the subtle undercurrent of depression fade until we left the area.

We still wonder about it now. Did we pick up anything from the underlying rock strata? Or did we absorb energies from the massed souls who had been drowned there in the previous century? Or were the Spirits of the Land here antagonistic to what they must have sensed around me? Or was it just that our place was haunted? It had some tenuous link with C.S. Lewis but there was no record of any haunting. The house we stayed in didn't *feel* malign. The nearest I got to
Otherness was when I was struck by the thin waning Moon as it threw red light on me at 4am, with the attendant bright star that I assume was Venus. I should know such things, but I don't. I'm not being falsely modest when I describe myself as a second-class intellectual and third rate academic. Thank the gods for Wikipedia is wot I say.

I tried some inner work toward Elphame but nothing sparked. M had a similar experience with regards to her own Work. There would have no point in chanting *Nevin Nevin Nevin*. The inner tribes in this area might have been offended. And there

81

was not the slightest hint of the 'pixie' I'd evoked the previous week. I thought about doing a ritual 'clearing' but decided that would have been irrelevant. It was almost like being in *The Truman Show*: nothing was quite real or relevant to me, no matter how perfect it looked.

I'm not saying that this was a Brigadoon-ish place, out of time. Go there yourself and you'll no doubt be stunned by its beauty and adore every moment. But M, with her very different Work, felt the same as me.

Hmmm...

I'm sure that you will all have similar experiences in your own areas. Another deadness for me has always been the town of Marlborough – the town of Merlin's Mound according to some. I should have thrummed with its energies when I visited it twice a month in my magnificent Mobile Library Van but I was always glad to get away. Dunno why.

A strange night... Although I tried to get the 'Star Window' to come alive, it was just a flat image before my brow. I've realised over many years that whenever I devise a technique for some practical inner Magick, it only seems to work for me personally the first time. After that, it's as though the whole process loses its energy. Others have used the techniques I've suggested over the years with great and continual success, so I feel a bit exasperated.

However, I've just had a turbulent time of it in the pre-dawn light, heralded by what I suppose was our fae-blackbird singing his heart out in our narrow street this time, rather than our long and narrow garden at the other side. I must have been out of my body and on a mission, because I found myself dealing with several earth-bound spirits at an unfamiliar but apparently haunted house. This was not a simple dream. Believe me, I dream in detail *every* night and remember most of them the next day, and they're invariably tedious and meaningless - little better than neuro-electrical discharges of trivia, if there is such a thing. Rubbish, in other words. This was different in tone and detail. I was fully myself, standing in darkness at the corner of the old house next to gardens.

The first earth-bound appeared and leered and menaced me with a hugely aggressive face much larger than his body. *You don't need to do that*, I said, with raised, admonishing finger. He stopped. His face became normal, human. Middle-aged and once-powerful but now scared. He was lost. I reminded him that he was *not* alone, that he should look back into his own past to find someone he once loved. His face changed. He turned away from me and saw behind him smiling souls a-waiting. He went, sighing into his peace. Then there was a very small girl, perhaps four years old, and with insights from the back of my mind I somehow reminded her of, or summoned up, her grandparents, who were waiting for her with endless love and cuddles. I don't know why her Mum and Dad weren't there. Another soul emerged from the gardens around the house but the details of this one I forget. And finally there was an oddity involving a businessman, once smartly dressed but now tatty, whose life had been taken before he had signed an important contract. That single failure of signing the contract had stalled him. As my old Mam would have said he could neither 'heck nor gee' in this space between the worlds. At that moment M appeared next to me, cheerfully suggesting *we* create a contract for him and so we did, and we held up a big astral sheet of legalese and we three signed it on the dotted line and his relief was palpable, and he went.

And I awoke to Blackbird and the full light of dawn.

Was this the undercurrent of our strange holiday only a few days ago? Had we been assailed by troubled souls?

I don't know.

But I do know that both the bollard and the grocery cart have gone from the River Biss. Authorities from the local Waterways must have come and removed them. There was also a fella testing the quality of the water, but he was too busy for me to ask questions. The river is flowing beautifully now and almost looks attractive at that otherwise neglected little bridge, despite the major roadworks going on all around.

And my own flows of energy are pure and clear again and I whizzed around my Cardiac Rehab class this afternoon like an Olympic athlete. I even raced briefly with the delightful octogenarian lady we all call (affectionately and with huge respect) The Duracell Bunny. After the first three yards she just shot ahead.

It strikes me that in terms of 'Continuations', maybe she could be yet another aspect of the Queen of Elphame herself, showing the rest of us with damaged hearts how to live again, as the Deaf Queen I met earlier showed us other ways of communicating. This one also has an appropriate name but of course I can't blab that here. And are the rest of us a continuation of her Coven? And does she see me as Andro Man and want me to provide 35 babies?

NicNevin NicNevin NicNevin...

I'm in the library now. It's Friday. Freya's Day. It's also the day of Venus, a planet which is apparently very close to hearts of the Fae. And it's *also* 54 years since Neil Armstrong first set foot on the Moon. I was in a small shop in Bardon Mill at the time, where they had a telly set up. This was in a part of Northumberland that was also, as I later learned, in the heart of my great great great (many times) grannie's realm on the *paternal* side. I saw on-line that the shop, the only one in the very small village, is now up for sale.

The pc here keeps crashing and I wonder if it's something to do with this Work I'm attempting. Probably not, but it adds spice to my yarns

As I continue by simply scribbling in my notepad, I fancy creating a sort of spell that **will** transport you, the reader, toward that inexplicable Being known as Robert Kirk. This is another quantumish thing: if he is in my head then some sort of quantum particle is also bobbing about in yours. Think of him/it as an irritating midge: swat it away if it bothers you. Let me know how you all get on.

But first a brief note about Kirk himself…

The Very Reverend Robert Kirk [1644 – 1692] is known as the first person to translate the unholy bible into Gaelic, so that the Common Man (am I allowed to use that term?) could could access it without needing priests. But despite this major and hugely laudable achievement he is now best known for his book *The Secret Commonwealth of Elves, Fauns, and Fairies written* in 1691. In this extraordinary piece of work Kirk tells stories about folk (including himself) who had contact with faeries.

How did he describe them?

'These Siths or Fairies they call Sleagh Maith or the Good People ... are said to be of middle nature between Man and Angel, as were Daemons thought to be of old; of intelligent fluidous Spirits, and light changeable bodies (lyke those called Astral) somewhat of the nature of a condensed cloud, and best seen in twilight. These bodies be so pliable through the sublety of Spirits that agitate them, that they can make them appear or disappear at pleasure.'

He sought to investigate the Siths and learn about them. He believed in their reality and felt that they could be investigated and perhaps incorporated into the Christian faith. In his research he collected several personal accounts and stories of those who claimed to have encountered them.

The faery nexus (good word that!) in Aberfoyle was on Doon Hill, or Dun Shi, also known as 'Fairy Knowe' or 'Dun Sithean', a short walk from his house, the Manse. It strikes me, pleasingly, that his strolls there seemed to have been like mine have become across Trowbridge, with much the same aim. I begin to wonder if I might now find a physical 'Continuation' of this hill, my own 'Secret Commonwealth' in this area? I suppose this must be Cley Hill, home of the King of Faeries known hereabouts as Bugley, from the variants Bwwca, Pooka, Puck, Pook.[12]

Anyway... one night in May 1692, the Rev. Kirk shamefully left his pregnant wife alone and went out for a walk to the hill, clad only in his nightshirt, clearly entranced. Some people found him there and brought him home where he died. This was probably a simple heart attack although it was whispered among us Humans that it might have been the result of 'elf-shot', that is, caused by elves shooting invisible elf-arrows at a person. It was felt that the Good People were angry with him for going into the domain of the Unseelie Court, where he had been warned not to go, and decided to imprison him in the hill.

However, it was whispered by some that he actually didn't die but had been carried away by the Siths, the faeries, and that his grave contained a 'fetch', a replica, or just a pile of stones.

---

12 See my *Short Circuits*. And also *Neurolithica*.

Shortly after this Kirk appeared as a vision in front of his cousin, Graham of Duchray. He told him that he was not dead and that he would appear at the christening of his (Kirk's) child. When he appeared as promised, Graham was to throw an iron dagger at Kirk and this would release him from captivity, as it was (and is) well known that faeries don't like iron. Understandably, poor Graham was too scared to do this and the moment was lost.

And so it is believed that the Reverend Robert Kirk's soul is still inside the lone Scots Pine tree on Doon Hill where visitors today write their wishes on pieces of white silk, or other white cloth, and tie them to the branches of the trees for the Good People to grant.

And later the Manse, from which he set off, became known as the place where Sir Walter Scott wrote his famous poem *The Lady of the Lake*, inspired perhaps by Nimue, or several scribal variants such as Ninianne and Viviane. Faery Women all. In fact that poem had every Faery theme you might want: wild huntsmen, dream-ladies, hermits, sacred kings, clan loyalties, liminal fords and mystick lakes, madness, the witchy Earl Bothwell and a bard called Allan!

It might have been Scott (a Freemason) who commissioned the later gravestone bearing the symbols of a *Thistle*, for Scotland, a large *Dagger* (that some argue is a Templar sword!), and a *Shepherd's Crook* for his mission. It seems there are lots of adjoining graves bearing

Masonic symbols in that graveyard, including an adjoining one with a cat's-head Green Man on it.

What a gripping story the Reverend Robert Kirk gives us, is what I say! But I'm becoming aware, yet again, that Kirk is a very powerful Vortex in anyone's life, and once you start to swirl around with him it's hard to escape.

Sorry 'bout that.

(I'm not sure what 'Lloyd' would make of all this about Kirk. I'd almost forgotten *him!* Remember? That cutesy little leprechaun from Central Casting who wanted to work with us Humans. Now, after flowing into the alternative realities of my own private Elphame, I'm not sure if 'Lloyd' was not just a delightful but useful fiction, up there with Don Juan Matus or Koot Hoomi – and also, I have to admit, those many imaginal Beings who have floated into my mind recently.)

So what is the 'Unseelie Court' that Kirk shouldn't have tried to enter?

There is some dispute about this. The *Unseelie* Court seems to relate to the the darkly-inclined faeries, who are un-blessed and un-holy. They were easily offended and they were seen as closely allied with witches. Unseelies venerate death (autumn and winter), whereas the *Seelies* venerate life (spring and summer) and all things beautiful and 'nice'. The only thing that seems to tie them together is a love of nature.

I've heard something of this from modern magicians who have had brief faery contacts. Not all of them like Humans or want anything to do with us. I suppose being Seelie or UnSeelie is relative: it must be the same as a Human traveling to a new town. The locals aren't necessarily going to like you and may well seem hostile unless they can sense something in common. When I lived in Hong Kong I was the giant *gwai-lo* from Tin-Hau Temple Road and the hostility was sometimes palpable. Yet they were perfectly decent people who came to enjoy my pitiful attempts at Cantonese and over-praised my burgeoning skills with chop-sticks.

Now... What has any of this Journal to do with Kirk? I suppose it's all to do with the ripples, or the flow. Throw a stone into your own personal River Biss and although the ripples might seem unconnected, they all flow outward from the same centre. That's not the deepest of philosophies, I know, but I'm not trying to become a deep philosopher like David Conway, if only because I'd never have the last word as he always does.

I'm not sure if my present inner ripples are to do with Spirit(s) of Place or the energies of that goddess known variously as Sulis, or Sulis-Minerva or even the much later near-corrupted but still potent local form of 'Saint' Katherine – she of the Wheel. [13]

As one of those ripples, I should first mention *John Wood the Elder* [1704 – 1754], a cheery looking fella who built Prior Park as his starter project and who was probably quite mad by the standards of the time. Yet he must have known more about and handled the true Inner Stuff

13 See *Searching for Sulis* by me and Margaret...

than most of us will ever grasp. Bear with me for a moment as this isn't quite the diversion it might appear…

Whole books have been written about the codes and teachings John  Wood the Elder seems to have built into his architecture, especially The Circus and the Royal Crescent – the Sun and Moon writ large amid the honey stone of the city that lies within the seven hills and nurtures the warm, bubbling sacred waters that drew the Romans there to marvel, slaughter and usurp.

John Wood, I was surprised to learn, was born in Twerton, which is a very 'Trowbridgean' part of Bath that attracts the same sort of jokes about the inhabitants from the same sort of snobs. (I once spent several years working in Twerton with Deaf and Deaf-Blind people – just sayin'.) He surveyed Stonehenge and Stanton Drew when no-one gave a toss about them except to rob their stone, and wrote extensively about King Bladud (a founder of Bath), arguing that this was actually the legendary Master Magician known across the continent as Abaris – whom you might want to Google for yourself. If you do, watch out for the ripples when *that* stone hits the waters of the Universal Mind. You don't have to make a trip to find these things out for yourself. You ARE here, now, as per the formulae given by *The Chariot*.

I'm babbling. Splashing. Rippling. *Kirk Kirk Kirk…*

Somehow, out of the blue, sometime in 1993 it must have been, and brooding on the Mysteries of Bath, I became aware of Robert Kirk. He was on horseback at the time. This makes no sense whatsoever, but I can only tell you what I saw/imagined/intuited/envisioned or just plain invented.

I had the mad impulse to write a novel called *The Giftie* about a time-travelling Robert Kirk who somehow manifested – in the flesh – in the City of Bath, on the street between John Wood's Circus and

Royal Crescent. It was really a visceral novel about madness and perception and faery and love. Me and my late friend Mark Colmar also did a script in which we saw that fine actor Billy Connolly playing Kirk's role. We had all sorts of adventures in the outer world trying to get the script accepted. We met production companies, directors (I could name names), financiers (two dodgy, one sincere) actors, musicians, film companies and agents, etc. etc. but at the last moment it all disappeared and it was deja-vu and Faery Gold all over again.

I also learned by chance that when I was writing *The Giftie*, R.J. Stewart, also of Bath, was writing his excellent non-fiction *Walker Between the Worlds* which was all about Kirk and contained the whole text of the 'Secret Commonwealth' with Stewart's unique commentary. Oh and a tidal wave of other synchronicities occurred that seemed to be of the 'signs following' sort, evidence that *something* was needed by inner plane energies and beings.

Yet somehow, whatever he is or wherever he walks today in whatever Realm, 'Robert Kirk' brings his own Seelie Court into my world even now, the moment I start to muse upon him. I won't go into boring details, just take it on trust: all sorts of highly unusual and unlikely people appearing in highly unlikely circumstances. I promise, that as you read this and brood upon him/it/them, the same will happen to you.

Apparently it's Terence Stamp's birthday today. Half a dozen people on Facebook are posting with various stupid *gifs*. Poor bugger… Clark Gable is remembered for *Frankly my dear, I don't give a damn*; Humphrey Bogart for his *Play it again Sam*; Clint Eastwood for *Go ahead, make my day*, but the immeasurably finer actor Terence Stamp is largely known for *Kneel Before Zod!*

Anyway, tonight we're going to Bath, which is our nearest big town. We've been invited to join friends for a performance of the *Magic of Figaro* at Prior Park college. It's not really my sort of thing, as I'm unapologetically low-brow, but they're a nice couple and it would be churlish of me to make excuses. Besides M always loves live musick. [14]

---

14 M tell me that it's the **Marriage** of Figaro.

So it's Bath that you must follow me toward, riding on the witch's broom of my imagination, soaring above the seven hills that surround Bath and then plummeting down to a glistening vagina-like crack between two of them that contains a small, lake, deer, and the college itself in a clitoral position at the head of the valley. That must seem crude, but how else can compare the shape of this glistening valley within valleys?

The Marriage of Figaro… Next time I'll give my ticket to David Conway and he can do the *Diva,* as I fancy only he can. It was described as a 'comic light opera' according to the £2.00 programme. For me, whose low-brows went so deep that they connected to my lizard-brain and made my prehensile tail twitch on the hard (expensive) seat and also impacted on my hearing, I might as well have sat next to the huge machine with sirens blaring that my daughter Jade drives as a Fire-fighter. (This is the little girl who was once a Continuation of 'Barbie'.) I might have had a *slight* hint of John Wood the Elder as we walked from the car park to the theatre past the Palladian architecture of buildings that were possibly inspired by Abaris, but if any of the Gentry were in my psyche before, they were certainly driven out that evening.

After, home and quiet, I had a very disturbed night with an endless dream… I struggled to protect M from a complete nutter who was obsessed with her and tried to keep her imprisoned. This was a simple Bad Dream, folks, nothing to do with High Jinks on the astral. I half-woke up, still in the clutches of torment and M still endangered. Normally, with all such troubled dreams, I would go back into the images and recast them to my advantage with great and elegant wisdom that Prince Harry might espouse these days as a Chief Impact Officer in California. But because there is only so much you can do with such guff or even potent Banishing Rituals, this time I went back into my dream with a self-created length of lead piping and beat the shit out of the lunatic while yelling *Kneel Before Zod you sod!* and freed M. instantly.

I think NicNevin might have approved…

M woke the next morning without ever knowing how brave I had been.

I'm in Coffee #1 now after a brisk stroll across town to get my steps in. So far I've done 7,400.

I had an odd encounter on the way, though. As I was crossing the main bridge across the Biss (the one with the old Victorian lock-up) I was politely stopped by a large-ish, poorly dressed and somewhat puzzled, overweight, middling-aged man with a helmet of lank, fair hair, wearing a large off-white nylon shirt and carrying a full plastic carrier bag in each hand.

Do you know Trowbridge? he asked, rather oddly in tone.

Not intimately, says I, quick as a flash but a rather cowardly one.

What's going on there? he asked, half-turning, arms still held by his side by the weight of the bags and nodding back toward the site of the old Bowyers factory. *What's going on? They used to be mills.*

I wasn't sure about this but didn't want to get into an argument about Mill Buildings v. the Sausage Factory that I knew for certain was there in my time. I thought the Mills were back in the Victorian era.

It's a wasteland, he said.

They have plans, I assured him. *They promise every year to renew.*

I was in a hurry. I didn't want a sub-Socratic dialogue. I gave him a bland smile and walked on, brisker than before, aiming for my mystickal 10K. He called something after me, toward my disappearing back, but I didn't quite catch the words. When I turned, he had gone.

It's only now in the caff that I wonder *Who* that was. Or even – ridiculously – who he thought *I* was. Didn't the questing knights have to ask the Fisher King (he with the damaged bollocks) what the meaning of the Wasteland was? I know that in some versions it's important NOT to ask the Fisher King its meaning.

Had I just met a continuation of Galahad or Perceval or one of the other prancing prigs? Well, I'm not interested. I don't want to get sucked into the vortex of the tupperware Grail Mysteries where all the holier-than-thou pricks amid their singing virgins bugger off to heaven and leave the rest of humanity behind. [15]

---

15 See more of my Grail spleen in *Short Circuits.*

More Kirk… He doesn't seem to want to leave me. I realise that I might not have liked like the actual fella if I'd met him in his lifetime. I think I did him a favour by making into a sexual athlete in *The Giftie,* in the form of Billy Connolly, rather than letting him priest away as the dour lowlander he must have been. I mean to say, if he translated his bible (lower case please) into Gaelic then he must have been aware of what a dreadful document it is, except for a very few brief moments of decency in the New Bits.

Hmmm...

The Reverend was of the opinion that the Invisible Folk are the spirits of the deceased. As the dead leave their bodies he felt that they may be diverted into this realm of the Fae and could remain there for many years.

So far so good. I understand that - sort of.

He argued that these Invisible Folk are indigenous to every land, including America, and preceded Human settlement in all the countries where Humans now live. Faery folk formerly practised agriculture on the surface of the earth, but when us Humans came we took possession of their land and drove them away. And so they came to be living underground, in faery hills, and in shadows - or else in marginal areas of Human society In some of these societies, the Invisible Folk adopted the manner of dress and the language of the occupiers.

Hah – 'marginal areas of Human society' says he. Like Trowbridge? Is *that* why I'm here!?

But I love his *next* idea…

Faeries, he explains, often appear in the form of specific Human Beings, giving the impression that the same person is in two places at the same time. This happens so often that Kirk cites the belief that there is a 'double' in the subterranean community for every human who lives on the Earth. He calls these apparent doubles 'Doublemen' or 'Co-Walkers'. In some instances, the 'Doubleman' has taken over the life of the person he resembles in an act of supernatural identity theft. Kirk then takes this idea of the double further, noting that there is a double of every living creature on earth that lives "In some other element'.

The faery world, in his marvellous view, is a sort of etherial mirror version of the physical world.

I write this now in the garden office. After an hour lopping branches off trees (after asking our dryad's permission but not waiting to hear it given), it is now pissing down outside. Yet but I'm dry in here and quite thrumming with that last bit of Kirkiana. I don't understand it at all, but I'm rather enchanted.

Thrum thrum thrum.

I don't need to do more than that now. I doubt if intellect and logic alone will get me into Elphame. If anyone can explain it to me in terms that Smiffy of the Bash Street Kids could understand then please write.

Yet… How does Kirk's take on faeries compare with what Guinevere told Wendy Berg? And how does Lloyd Leprechaun's inner-world view compare with Kirk or Berg?

I'm not sure that I need to juggle these differing insights in order to make sense. I'm beginning to suspect that 'making sense' of Faery is the last thing I should attempt because they'd turn it inside out and invert everything in any case.

Perhaps the Elphame that seems to flow over Northern England and Eastern Scotland is as different to the other Elven Realms as, say, Ireland is from Iceland?

I'm babbling coz I'm very tired. I blame Figaro. I need to go nap.

I'm scribbling this in a café in the basement of the small and crumbling Castle Place complex in Trowbridge that might soon be condemned. A few years ago this was the refuge of a small and crumbling and increasingly elderly Deaf community who would meet there. They chose it because it was cheap, as many deaf people are unemployed and sometimes unemployable. Some of them, also, could apply for State Benefits but they wouldn't; in their eyes they are *not* disabled and it's the Hearing People, they argue (with many dismissive and very rude signs), who should learn to communicate. I can't say I disagree.

Today, however, it has been taken over by a Turkish family and given a Turkish name that, for the moment, eludes me. With a few exotic extras it is more or less the same place but with a larger 'greasy spoon' type menu. Posh folk would sneer at the place but I quite like it, and will come more often. I'm sitting at a spacious table looking out onto the park, where I still wonder if any of the magnificent trees are faery hawthorns. I've got Coleston Brown's marvellous, illustrated book of Faery sigils in my backpack that I haven't yet opened to re-re-read, and also a tiny, dense book on the Holy Grail that insists the actual item is a silver chalice in Lincoln Cathedral. At least I *think* that's where the author argues. I haven't got that far yet. I mainly bought it, second-hand for 40 pence, because the blurb was quite matter-of-fact, non-esoteric, and another dig at all those who drool over the many alternatives.

Apparently this 'Castle Place' was built on the site of the original castle belonging to Humphrey de Bohun, whose wife was Maud de

 Lusignan. Now that very name ' Lusignan' made my senses prickle many years ago when I read Gareth Knight's *The Book of Melusine of Lusignon,* about the faery tradition that had grown up around her. Basil/Gareth told me that the faeries themselves made him learn medieval French when he was older than I am now, in order to access near-forgotten faery traditions and energies and awaken them today.

Maybe there's something going on with respect to Trowbridge at magico-historical levels that I might never fully understand…

And perhaps even such a downbeat café as this is also one of those 'marginal places' on the fringes of society that I mentioned earlier.

However, I babble again. I know of old that the faery Melusine can grab you and take you where you don't want or need to go. Besides, those lines of Kirk's about the 'Doubleman' are bothering me. So I suppose have to mention Kaspar O'Malley…

Kaspar told his own story in the first person in a novel I wrote in 2018 called *Twisted Light.* While playing in a ruined church just after the War, young Kaspar was almost killed when an old bomb blew up. It damaged and deformed his body and twisted his face, but also gave him a staggering, wild talent for Remote Viewing – and later Remote Influencing. He was taken in hand by a certain Colonel Waghorn of MI5 who gave him sanctuary in a house off the Imber Road in the small village of Bratton, on the northern edge of Salisbury Plain. This is a very real village only a five miles from Trowbridge; ; an easy walk on level ground or a quick drive with several (pleasing to me) Twenty-is-Plenty zones. It is often the start of some of our favourite walks along the high edges of Salisbury Plain. So Kaspar tells his story about those odd days and also later, when he moved to London, of his experiences among the nascent rock gods and gangsters of the 1960s, and finally to his retirement back in Bratton, wheelchair-bound by now but well looked-after by his two devoted female carers.

Shortly after I'd published this excellent novel to resounding indifference, M and I were in Bratton and making our way toward the faery ponds at Luccombe's Bottom when two young female carers appeared from Church Lane pushing a *very* elderly man in a wheelchair who was twisted and scarred and beaming with delight - as Kaspar invariably did.

Hello, I gasped, and he nodded back, smiling as if he were my oldest friend and knew all my secrets, and was enjoying a huge joke. Somehow this very old man knew me, he really did! It was one of those moments when Time and Reality was suspended. The trio moved on and turned a corner out of sight. They may have disappeared through a wormhole or a parallel world, I really don't know, I didn't think to follow them. I just stood there, somewhat stunned.

Yes Yes Yes I know that in that moment I *should* have, *could* have, done or *said* all sorts of things but I was so surprised that the moment was lost and was perhaps meant to be lost.

That's Kaspar O'Malley I whispered to M, and she agreed. I was still thrumming when we got to the faery ponds, which are just beyond the house I had written up as having been Kaspar's, though it was now, in reality, owned by one of Prince Harry's best friends forever.

Was Kaspar a *tulpa*? Or was he, somehow, a Doubleman? Or a manifestation of a parallel life? Or had I just fluked into Remote Viewing a near-contemporary while intending to write a novel about Boudicca?

(Let me know what you think. And purchase at least one copy of *Twisted Light* to try and reach a full coven of buyers.)

Plus I've sometimes thought that there is a sort of 'intra' class of people who seem to be independent of the rest of us in British society.

They're entirely and totally Human (I think) and while they live and work and relate within this world they are not actually *of* it. Those two carers were of that ilk, I feel certain. Over the years I've met others, self-employed in the Caring Professions, who are here in the world but not *quite* here.

Actually I sometimes think this is true of M also, but don't tell her.

That encounter was five years ago, though somehow it seems like a lifetime. Yet as recently as last year I spoke to someone with impeccable credentials who told me that the main drift of my implausible yarn was largely accurate; that Remote Viewing has been used with effect within the British Intelligence communities, although they will always deny it.

But then they would, wouldn't they?

Hmmm…

It's Monday now. I go to my Cardiac Coven in the afternoon but I'm scribbling in the Atrium this morning. After musing all yesterday and into the evening about that powerful and inexplicable experience at Bratton, I wake to find that overnight a crop circle has appeared there! I can only wonder if, to skew my previous comment… *maybe there's also something going on at magico-**geographical** levels that I might never fully understand.*

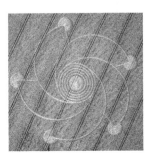

If some or even most of the crop circles are made by teams of humans working by dead of night, I believe that they are being influenced by intelligent energies/beings from the inner planes. I know someone who made a small circle decades ago at the beginning of the 'craze', if it might be called that. She *had* to do it; felt totally compelled by something deep within her soul that was connected with the land.

I think the crop circle shape that appeared last night at Bratton is akin to the sigils in Coleston Brown's book that I'm *still* carrying around with me without yet opening it. Maybe the faery sigils are working away without need for my brain to engage!

Nice thought, if a bit wacky.

Something about the Spirit of Place (and the Fae?) must want something from me. The synchronicity certainly seems to be something of a 'nudge'. *Bratton Bratton Bratton…*

On the other hand M, who is doing her own Work at very deep levels indeed, also feels that there are Spirit of Placey things going on relating to Trowbridge and its folks that are constantly surprising and sometimes startling.

Hmmm Hmmm Hmmm...

I know it's Tuesday today because the Wild Hunt in the shape of the U3A is just pouring out of the library on their group walk to god-knows-where. For all I know they could be marching into a trans-dimensional portal and exploring the Great Rift in the Milky Way. Or else I might find that if I ask questions about them at the Enquiry Desk I'll get funny looks and be told they don't exist at all.

On the other hand there is a large sign on display in the Atrium saying that the new café will be opening next week. About time, is wot I say, as two other cafés in town have recently closed.

I made a bit of a tit of myself in the Cardiac Coven Class yesterday. As I think I mentioned, they all warm up before the circuit training by briskly walking *widdershins* around the hall. No-one orders them in that direction but they just whizz, en masse. This time, before they started, I made some weak joke about being a rebel and set off *deosil*, hoping that the Coven would all laugh and join me, the new magister.

Not a chance. When the instructor arrived the whole group was marching one way and I was continuing opposite, dodging the flow when necessary. He must have thought me a twat.

I think this next will be Elphame related, somehow, so bear with me.

I've recently noticed an oddity about my mind that I suspect is quite common to most people, if unrecognised. Thus...

I lie in bed before sleep, untroubled, sinking into a gentle and flowing reverie that has no significance and needs no analyses. Then, to get slightly more comfortable and enter Nod completely, I turn from my back onto my left side. A mere 90°. Yet my mind instantly flows into a completely different reverie that has no relation to the first. It's not that the images are connected or begin from scratch: I'm gently aware that the new story-line has already been flowing and now carries on with completely different scenes and themes that I'm also part of, in a differing way. This is hard to describe. I suppose it's like turning on the car radio halfway into a song and then, at the press of a button, connecting with a completely different and equally unexpected song.

By turning on my side do I connect with the reveries of my parallel Self?

Is this line of consciousness lying alongside my evryday one what Kirk means by the Co-walker.

And does Elphame exist within me - and you - but at 90° to 'normal' awareness?

I haven't glimpsed that *Aos Sí* or pixie again, although I can remember his/it/they/her quite clearly: elfin, pure-white almost translucent flesh, ethereal; pure pure pure and very small. Then again that 'Star Mirror' I fashioned has definitely proved to be another spiritual OTP, a One Time Password of the sort I'm constantly creating, as I think I confessed.

Bit worried about the internal 'Mab Stone'. I still haven't got a date for it's removal, and I'm not yet at the faery-story *year-and-a-day* following the heart attack, after which they will consider removing it. That's worrying me more than the cardiac arrest itself, as I was largely out of it in the helicopter off the Isle of Wight, whereas problems following the removal of the first bladder stone here in Trowbridge had me screaming. I can't really relax until I know it's done. I've heard about Faery Healing and wish I could get some.

There must be a thousand on-line sources and a million actual books that point out something about the Northern Witches of 'Elphamia' that I've only just realised… Those poor souls who had been burned at the stake never saw themselves as 'witches'; they were, in their own minds, healers. Especially healers who learned their skills from faeries – whatever they might be.

In this respect, flowing on, the Google Angel (who has now largely replaced the Library Angel in my life), keeps pointing out that Water and its ability to heal disease was often associated with faeries and thus the 'witches' who communed with them. It seems that south-flowing water was deemed particularly special.

There is a lovely site *https://britishfairies.wordpress.com* that goes into detail about this:

> Katharine Craigie, who was tried on Orkney in 1640, had told a sick man that she could discover whether he was afflicted by 'ane hill spirit, a kirk spirit or a water spirit', which are probably different types of trow. She did this by placing three stones in the household's fire all day; these were then left under the house's threshold overnight and, in the morning, were dropped separately into a bucket of water. The stone that 'chirned and chirled' when it was dropped in the water indicated that a kirk spirit (probably a trow living in a nearby church yard) was the cause of the malady.

Others used this same technique to diagnose afflictions caused by hill spirits and sea spirits. James Knarstoun, in 1633 also used three stones for the same purpose, bringing one from the shoreline, one from a hill (surely a fairy knoll) and one from a kirk yard, and promised that once the spirit was revealed, it could be 'called home again'.

I can't help but think of modern homeopaths when I read about these treatments.

And then there was Isobell Strauthaquinn was tried for witchcraft in 1597. She learned her healing skills from her mother who in turn had been taught them from her fairy lover. Isobell was accused of curing people with water in which the bones of the dead had been washed.

It strikes me that the River Biss is south-flowing but I'm hardly likely to scoop any of it because it would have flowed over the rusting ribs of dead grocery carts and immortal plastic bollards.

And then there were the three women from Perth in Scotland: Isobel Haldane, Janet Trall and Margaret Hormscleugh, who were also accused of witchcraft on account of the healing they did for the common folk. Perth, it should be noted, is known to have been occupied ever since Mesolithic hunter-gatherers arrived there more than 8,000 years ago. Nearby Neolithic standing stones and circles date from about 4,000 BC, a period that followed the introduction of farming into the area. This was clearly deep within the domain of Queen NicNevin and her tribe. These women also used south-flowing water in their spells and charms and potions, and all claimed to learn their skills from visiting faeries in the hills around Perth.

Those who used water in various ways for diagnoses knew that it swirls clock-wise for health, anti-clockwise for death.

Of course an awful lot has been written (not least by me) about Masaru Emoto, a Japanese businessman, author and pseudoscientist who claimed that human consciousness could affect the molecular structure of water. His 2004 book *The Hidden Messages in Water* was a New York Times best seller. I used these ideas a lot in *Searching for Sulis* and was impelled to write a full novel called *du Lac* (the clue is in the name) giving a modern slant on a very powerful faery contact.

Enough said. I'm getting tired.

It's a Friday now. Day of Venus. M is off for a walk with her pal on the edges of Salisbury Plain. I'm in the Atrium but a bit low again today because my own physical Mab Stone is bothering me. I just wish it could be gone. Still, my gloom is nothing that can't be cured by a cuppa tea, a good book, and a brief nap like a little baby. The NHS has saved my life many times, and I'm confident they will get me sorted over this once the year-and-a-day condition is met.

Beyond the Atrium, things seem to be falling apart in Trowbridge as a whole though. At the northern end of the park the large pond/small lake that was once lively with swans, ducks and a spouting fountain is now drained. Apparently the liner became torn and would now cost huge sums to repair. Plus our quirky Town Hall has just closed for the next two years in order to be completely refurbished and turned into a musickal centre par excellence. What with the closure of other businesses in the surrounding streets, the town centre will become even more of a Wasteland.

I become aware of an ageing but quite elegant gentleman to the left of me who seems keen to have a few words about this. He seems to have more substance than usual, and not just a Continuation.

> *Things fall apart; the centre cannot hold…*
> Oh do shut up, Will.
> *Surely some revelation is at hand…*
> We have the same glasses. Are yours from the Pound Shop too?

102

I feel a bit guilty dismissing him with a spirally twist of my hand that I learned from the late Paddy Slade, a hereditary witch from South Stoke near Bath; few people knew more about the *sidhe* than Yeats did, and he was a *real* Magician, up there with Mr Butler. But if he appears again in younger form I'll try to give him advice about Maude Gonne. It's odd, but last night I had a Facebook message out of the blue from the girl who first dumped me in 1971 for a devilishly handsome Olympic-class judoka and thus broke my young heart into pieces of passionate intensity. She changed me, changed me utterly, and a terribly ugly sort of beauty was born. Anyway, the girl apologised. Said she could never understand why she dumped me.

I wrestle with forgiveness. By that I mean forgiveness of things real or imagined that have been done to me; but equally with forgiveness of myself for the very real and *not* imagined things I've done to others.

However, perhaps because it's an End of Days things for us both I was able for once, with good grace to say that I really did forgive her. Besides, at the back of my mind I've long known that she did me a favour. Maybe it was the faeries that pushed her.

Odd Odd Odd… Things seem to be turning and twisting me in my own gyre at the moment.

Still, M is pleased with a piece someone sent her about Trowbridge. It was written years ago by a 'spiritual minister' who insisted that our dear and battered and crumbling Trowbridge is actually a major power point, with a convergence of up to 12 energy lines into the centre where it is awash with spirits. Also, she's been reading about the 'Michael and Mary Lines' of energy and consciousness that stretch some 350 km from the far west of Cornwall to the east coast of Norfolk. Hamish Miller and Paul Broadhurst made this famous with their influential book *The Sun and the Serpent*. During an epic trek to dowse the St Michael Alignment, the authors found the more subtle presence of a meandering Mary line, and discerned the existence of a long-lost science that harnessed the energies of the Earth and Sun at cross-quarter days to fertilise, nurture and purify the Earth. The Mary Line, they found, went right down the nave of St James Church in Trowbridge and thus, by dead reckoning, probably through our street if not across our long and narrow and sometimes uncanny garden.

The café is now open in the Atrium. Bliss Bliss Bliss. I bought the very first cuppa. They've undercharged me, I think, but I didn't tell them. I'll be good in future! That's probably what Andro Man and all the others said to their Inquisitors before they were condemned to death.

Yesterday, we drove out to Avebury. M has been learning about Dragon Energies in her own group and it seems that many such lines of force meet there within one of the circles. As we went around, we each did our own inner things. Although I brought up the imagery of the Fae at various stones I can't say that anything special happened, although the notion of 'Green Fire' kept floating in and out of my thoughts. Not really sure what that is. I don't really need to say anything more, beyond that we had a lovely day in among the 6000 year old stones.

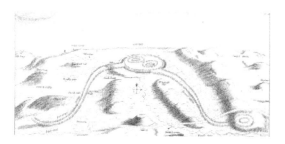

Today, though is another U3A day! And so it's Tuesday, a Mars day. (I have an irreverent memory of a telly jingle from my childhood that went 'A Mars a day helps you work, rest and play...' That was a chocolate bar of course. They still sell them. In Scotland, in the areas of Elphame, they Deep Fry them.) They're all congregating as I write and there's a lot collective giggling, such a cheerful group before they march out to declare war against ageing and unfitness. It's also, apparently, the day of the Lion's Gate Portal opening. That is, August 8th. This marks the alignment of the sun Leo, the star Sirius, the constellation of Orion's Belt and presumably also dear old Trowbridge in Wiltshire. I wrote about that at length somewhere but I've largely forgotten, so it's not important.

Apparently this is a day for Manifesting. Do I want to Manifest anything? Apart from the underlying and universal wish for Health, Wealth and Happiness for me and M and all our family, there are only three books that I want, an updated Hearing Aid and perhaps some large reading glasses. I suppose I'm pretty much sorted. Of course there are endless numbers of Places near and far that I want to visit but I can't make plans until I've had the operation to remove the Mab Stone.

I will be cautious though. I do think that when a person believes that he nothing left to learn and cannot be taught anything new, then he is called Home. I've known a few people like that over the decades. And of course I've still got this teeny tiny niggling worry that when I finish 'Elphame' I'll have served my purpose.

I did mutter my usual *NicNeven NicNeven NicNeven* chant as I walked into town first thing, but I don't think Neven and this particular Portal are a good mix.

Anyway, I've just dipped into Coleston Brown's book on Faery Sigils that I've been carrying everywhere with me (along with my survival kit of stuff to use if I have another heart attack). As the U3A thundered out I asked the Fae to give me a sigil and opened the book at random, eyes closed (as you do) and I was given Bo'ah.

Hmmm… This is known as *The Wizard's House. The Hut.* And the text tells me that *Bo'ah* indicates lineage, spiritual heritage, Otherworld Teachers and Wayshowers, adding 'The sigil itself is suggestive of early meander signs. A Human landscape expressing Faery'.

Well, I can't argue with any of that can I? And there is more…

'Thus the sigil relates to one's Way to wholeness, where faery, human and Green Fire are harmoniously expressed and embodied.'

As the for the 'Magical Applications' it suggests:

- Connecting with ancestral powers and presences
- Awakening the Faery Covenant
- Tuning Human activity with Faery
- Building bridges across Time
- Reconnecting the Covenant
- Genetic magic

Really, this seems to be totally in tune with what I've been attempting. I won't muddy the waters by looking at other sigils yet. It suggests to me at least the swirls and whirls I've been looking at in the River Biss. At times it has seemed that my life has been a series of incidents – living pixels – around which a pattern seems to form. Maybe the pattern is Bo'ah?

NicNeven NicNeven NicNeven...

I can't say the opening of the Lion Gate had any effect upon me though M. did some very deep Work of her own in that respect. But today, the 12th of August, is a curious case of Hatched, Matched and Despatched. I should mention first, though, that after being M's groupy and watching her in the *Rock Choir* on Fore Street, in Trowbridge, we had a celebratory lunch afterward at the Mill at Rode. I was about to babble to her about those principles when the waitress (am I still allowed to use that term?) apologised for the slight delay in serving us because a Kingfisher had become trapped in one of the water channels of the Mill itself.

These are, of course, rarely seen birds and deeply symbolic.

You have to rescue it first, I insisted. *That's an important bird, you know.*

We will. And I know, she said, and shot off.

The bird was freed and I was able to yarn to M about about how August the 12th was the date of Helena Blavatsky's birth; the marriage of Aleister Crowley and Rose; and the death of William Blake. Anyone reading this book will need no explanation about those people, though I would point out that it was Rose who helped channel *Liber Al* into the world, yet she is too often written off as Crowley's dipsomaniac failure of a wife.

Bless bless bless...

Cheers to all, I said to M. as we clinked our glasses, me being terse, aware of the flow of the River Frome beneath our feet and the roar of waters in the mill race. Someone had sent me a quote from Charles Leland's book on *Gypsy Sorcery*, written in 1891, that seemed appropriate for the moment. It was about what he called the *'sweet old sorcery'* and went:

> But nature is eternal, and while grass grows and rivers run, man is ever likely to fall again into the eternal enchantments. And truly until he does, he will have no new poetry, no fresh art, and must go on copying old ideas and having wretchedly worn-out exhibitions in which there is not one original idea.

I've always tried to be original in everything I've written, even at risk of seeming banal. I've no doubt that someone reading this simple, non-scholarly, highly-personal manuscript on Elphame will pull it apart like the wings off a butterfly.

Cheers to all, I say again as the cod and chips arrive and the waitress smiles happily at having rescued the magick kingfisher.

The Atrium. I noticed on the way here taking the long route across town, there are now *three* bollards in the River Biss. I wonder if they're breeding.

Today is the first anniversary of my heart-attack and the subsequent spectacular flight by heli-ambulance from the Isle of Wight to Southampton Hospital that is, providentially, a 'Centre of Excellence' for heart conditions. Apart from occasionally pissing blood caused by the Mab Stone, I'm probably better than I have been for some years.

It has only just struck me that the term 'Wight' is often used as another name for elves. Although the Islanders themselves don't accept this etymology it's entirely appropriate for me just now. Thus a wight (wicht in Scots) can either be a human or some supernatural being, typically of the faery family, but can also encompass ghosts and a whole range of other spirits.

I've been having Deep Thoughts about my Cardiac Class – or Cardiac Coven as I secretly think of it, that I go to every Moon Day. There is a circuit of a dozen different exercises we do in the large gym, carrying a 5kg weight in each hand. Following an orchestrated warm-up by Andy to musick, we then do individual one minute timed-exercises in lifting and hefting, stepping and bending, wall push-ups and various twists and leg curls. And at a certain point in the circuit the option is to walk briskly around the room - or jog. So far the only joggers have been the women, all of whom are a decade older than me. For the first time last week I had the confidence to actually break into a run at this point, although I could hardly describe my motion as gazelle-like. During all of them I've never had Neven and Co. far from my thoughts. The instructor noticed this and asked me (rather tetchily I thought) if my mind was *really* on the regime, and if I was simply going through the motions with ill grace.

What could I say? Well, two possibilities:

- *Actually Andy, if I seem somewhat vacant it's because my thoughts are largely upon a coven of witches who were burnt at the stake some four centuries ago and 600 miles from here, because of their love for the Queen of Faery.*

Or…

- *Actually Andy the truth is I really **don't** want to be there, but I do understand the importance of this Work and will keep coming and not give up.*

Somehow I made him laugh and gained an admirer by teaching him British Sign Language for 'Fuck Knows' (make a circle out of your thumb and forefinger and jab it vigorously back and forth upon the tip of your nose).

At the beginning, before we all start, I've given up trying to get them to circle *deosil*. Yet the whole sequence has given me a Cunning Plan, as Baldrick might say. What if I identify each place on the circuit with one of those healers who were burned as witches? I think Catholics do that with the Stations of the Cross don't they? I'll give that some thought and make it happen in some shape or form. So I suppose their determined circuits *widdershins* might be entirely apt.

And what if all the people in those group are 'Continuations' of NicNeven's coven? What if they are, somehow, incarnations of one of the 35 children that Andro Man believed he had sired? (Listen, I don't care if Andro was, in reality (whatever that might mean!) a complete nutter. To take that attitude is to miss the point, if you ask me. So I'll have a good brood on this over the next few days and see if I can turn the circuit into an invoking or evoking ritual, with a coven Name at each stage and then giving it all power by my bursting into a run when I reach the appropriate point.

Not sure exactly how this might Work, but I'll let you know.

It's been a funny few days though. I've noticed that when I walk through town a (small) number of individuals nod and smile and give me quick, almost discreet waves as though we're old acquaintances. Yet I'm sure I've never met them before. Is a kind of 'Continuity Coven' forming in the this everyday world of mine? And has this been happening to you also, now I've made you think of it?

Not Likely says an amiable woman who has appeared on my right side this time, on the long grey sofa behind the café area.

I recognised her straight away of course, not least because I've got a copy *of Fortean Times* in my backpack with a long article about her.

Margaret Murray. You look…
Young? Not like the dry old stick and uber-crone?
 You created the rubric 'The Old Religion'.
And a good thing I did.
You are the grandmother of modern Wicca.

So mote it jolly well be!

I've always liked her books, especially *The Witch-Cult in Western Europe (1921)* and *The God of the Witches.* When I was 16 I founded the *Ashington Grammar Occult Society* (you'll have whispered of little else, I suppose, especially our legendary attempt to levitate our English teacher, Charles (Chaz) Lossasso). We tried to get our headmaster, the fearsome G.T.L. Chapman, to give us a grant to buy these books. He already had his own copy of the former but refused us any dosh, largely because one of the other requests was for A.E. Waite's *Book of Black Magic and Pacts* that he didn't think entirely relevant within the coal-mining atmospheres of Ashington.

I've known many Wiccans who took Murray's writings as a new, deliciously heretical Gospel and teased out of themselves and for themselves long, fantastical strands of spiral possibilities, like a sort of Inner DNA but much of it junk, infected with yarns, happenstances, ancestors, wild talents and delightful, harmless fibs - so mote them all be. I'd have done all this for myself decades ago if I could have found a young Wiccan priestess who fancied me.

The River Biss is very low today; the grocery cart (from Asda again) and bollards are prominent. I feel personally embarrassed, even though there is no-one else around. It is almost like a dirty secret (although I don't suppose I have too many of those left these days). And so...

I storm into the Atrium. Onto the pcs. I Google: Trowbridge; Town Hall; Rubbish Collection.

The relevant department looms out of the flat crystal ball. It is upstairs, in this very building.

I spend a little time in quiet corner of the Atrium (i.e. also in the chamber of my heart) and Assume the God-form of Horus, easily and powerfully, as I've worked with Him/It/They many times over many decades now. I pulsate with power. I am big, with manly chest, stout thews, great biceps and have the piercing vision of Hawks.

I mount the stairs to the Upper Rooms. My steps are thunderous, the world shakes. The requisite door is before me. I pound on it with my *uas* wand and it slams open against the wall, breaking plaster and revealing red brick. The lights in the small office flicker weirdly and the man behind the desk (a weedy human with pebble glasses and comb-over hair) quivers before me.

You, little man, **Will** *clear the River Biss. You will NOT REST until it is done.*

I will, he whimpered.

I might have exaggerated this just a little. In my Alternative World I *did* send the department a detailed email giving them clear directions as to where the cart and bollards are and I now await their reply. I need that rubbish gone to purify both the Biss and thus my localised earth-consciousness. I was told that the Council has a very large magnet that they will use, and I'm glad my tax is used in this way. I've always had a thing about magnets. If you ever want to buy me a present, buy me a magnet. Or a torch. Or best of all, an Amazon book token. (If I had a token from the local bookshop, it means I would have to ask the young and innocent assistant to order books with the VERY weird titles I invariably want and she might think me a swivel-eyed nutter[16].)

Assuming the God-form... This is always a useful technique. I'm not sure how self-professed magicians can do without it, but some of them do. If I really wanted to confront or challenge anyone, I'd be more likely to use Set instead of Horus.

This next short piece might seem far removed from NicNeven and her witch/healers in the realms of Elphame but bear with me for a moment...

_____

16 My eyes do not swivel, no matter what David Conway says.

Some years ago a seer who earnestly but quietly believed herself to be a reincarnation of Dion Fortune associated me with *Khasekhemwy* a pharaoh at the tail end of the little-known 2nd Dynasty, c. 2890 – c. 2686 BCE. As I explained at length in my earlier book 'Al-Khemy', I don't really have any personal investment in that historical figure other than to give my usual *Hmmm*.

Yet I was amiably taken by the fact that his name means 'The two powers have appeared', and is the only king to have selected a royal name that commemorates both Horus, the god traditionally associated with the living pharaoh, and Seth, or Set, his trickster brother. When I learned that Khasekhemwy was also the first pharaoh to depict both deities on his *serekh* (the stylized rectangular frame in which a king's 'Horus name' was displayed) I did feel a certain kinship. I've invoked his name many times since, but without any obvious result.

And again, years ago, during my 'Egyptian Phase' I was greatly taken with an oddity known as Set-Heru, or Darkness and Light conjoined. (Most magicians have their 'Egyptian' phases; it's almost like going through puberty.)

 Today, I have a sense of that symbol Bo-ah again. Remember? There seems to be a central line of 'flow' around which energies and events from future and past are twisting and spiralling. Or maybe that loose dot below the sigil is Me, observing. I expect everyone has days like this. I felt it strongly within my Cardiac Coven two days ago. I was mentally trying to assemble a ritual structure for future use, having noted that there definitely are *12* Stations around the room. Not more, not less. I wasn't sure last time. Should I associate these with the months of the year and thus work through the Seasons? And/or link each one with a member from Andro Man's original Coven?

So far, the names I've got that definitely connect with NicNeven are:

Alesoun Peirsoun
William Simpson
Andro Man
Bessie Dunlop
Marion Grant
Janet Horne
Major Thomas Weir
Jean Weir
Agnes Finnie
Lilias Adie

They were are probably not all part of the same coven at the same time, so I'll brood and Bo-ah myself back into them as I get more information. Or else just make it up as I go along, as I usually do – though I'm not in the same league as Castaneda or Hubbard or Sanders in that respect.

Yesterday though, as I worked around the Cardiac Coven Classroom doing all the exercises with weights, stretching, twisting, squatting, stepping, bending (with discreet farts), I came to the Station that required me to stroll/walk/ briskly-run around the entire Circuit for a whole minute. As I began lolloping around, quite proud of myself by this time, I heard the whisper:

What about me?
Eh?
(This wasn't clairaudience but more of an inflow of thought.)
*What about **me**?*
Who are you?
Christsondy.

I immediately remembered Andro Man's words, probably given under torture, when he spoke of NicNeven's husband who had this very odd name, given the context in which he told it.

Andro had first seen Christsondy as a boy and described him to his inquisitors as The Devil, who was also married to the Queen of Elphame herself. What struck me though was the powerful image of how he saw the Queen and her company riding white horses in the snow and Christsondy, the Devil himself, suddenly appeared in the form of a stag. All of these supernatural and possibly infernal beings had human shapes, said Andro, yet they were as shadows, 'playing and dancing whenever they pleased.' They were all shape-shifters, and the Queen herself could be old or young as she needed.

That powerful image of Christsondy emerging from the snow as a stag is not something I – or we - should ignore.

Pause for a moment and go to that glade yourself. Secret and Sacred places are glades of every kind. See, feel, the silence of the forest, the primeval trees heavy with snow, casting pale blue shadows from a fading lemon sun onto the thick white carpet beneath. Feel, see the silence and purity of an ancient realm in which you once travelled. In such a place, how can the stag of seven tines *not* appear before you. Be simple, be humble. Nod your acknowledgement. Accept whatever name you might be given. Or just whisper as I have been doing:

Christsondy, Christsondy, Christsondy.

And then*:*

Go away now I thought, as I made my way to the next Station of the gym.

It's a Bank Holiday next Monday so the Coven won't rejoin for a fortnight. I determined that next time I would Assume the God-Form of the Stag (or the Antlered Priest) as I try to raise the power of the circle in my widdershins circuits and chant his name in a peeping and muttering sort of way.

I wonder if Andy will notice...

In Andro Man's days of yore, and even into my lifetime, anything not obviously Christian and bursting with *Light Light Light* and more bloody *Light* was necessarily of the Dreadful Darkness and the Dirty

Devious Devil. And as I write this I'm now Bo-ahed again and seeing how patterns twist inward, time-travelling me yet again to the counter of a bookshop in Newcastle on Tyne in 1972. I was determined to buy the latest book by Francis X. King. Although I'd never met him he had always been supportive in his letters to a young whipper-snapper like myself and was one of the first writers to open the door into the history of Ritual Magic in England. I soaked up all the information he revealed about the Golden Dawn, the Stella Matutina, the Hermes Temple and Fraternity of the Inner Light and the rest. To me it was like lying down full length in a river of white fire and letting all these details flow and burn through me, yet also with the sense that, somehow, I already *knew* this stuff and that a part of me was already flameproof. I suppose it's like when you begin to research your family tree as I've been doing recently: they are dead names and unknown places, yet I know that these are all part of me and of how I Became - somewhere along that central line of Bo-ah.

So… long story short, I saved my money and took the bus to Newcastle and went to buy his latest learned treatise *Hermes and Eros*

only to find that the publisher (to Francis' horror and embarrassment) had renamed it, with suitably lurid cover, as *Sexuality, Magic and Perversions*. It's impossible to say this title out loud without putting the emphasis on the final word *Perversions* – or is that just me? I was horrified. Embarrassed. The world of Newcastle on Tyne in 1971 was still not as free and anything goes-ical as it soon became. Yet this was a Magickal Quest and I *had* to have the book.

The young girl behind the counter took my money but looked at me suspiciously; I looked away and my eyes definitely didn't swivel. She must have been projecting all sorts of darknesses upon me as if I was one of the pervs hinted at on the cover. *I'm only buying it for a friend,* I muttered. Under torture I'd have denied any knowledge of such things, or like Andro might have hinted that Christsondy was the Devil and nothing to do with a good little boy like me! I'd have blamed David Conway if he'd been around then. Perhaps he was. Is. *The Big Boy did it and ran way*, I'd have cried.

So I think that the Scottish inquisitors of 4000 years ago were likely to have been of the same ilk: Christsondy was *necessarily* The Devil; they didn't want to know that Darkness can be healing and good and necessary, so they tortured this gobby, garrulous, scruffy little Priest of the Devil called Andro Man because of his sexuality, magic and perversions.

Meanwhile, at the same moments in the beginning of Time in Khem, when Khasekhemwy left the throne, those who came after turned the purity of the Darkness represented by Set into similar notions of Him/It/They being a creature of Evil. Perhaps Set and Christsondy are one.

Does any of that make sense?

I'll get back to Elphame soon, honest. This is all getting a bit tiring, especially as I've now seen an old office chair rusting away in the Biss beyond the weir.

I am perplexed. Were they the last words of Aleister Crowley in his boarding house in Hastings or of George Armstrong Custer on the field of the Greasy Grass? I *am* perplexed though, and have been for a week since my last Cardiac Coven. After I had that brilliant idea of invoking Christsondy and Assuming his God Form at certain times and places, I assumed that doors to Elphame would at least creak open, or that visions of the Fae would burst upon me with as much clarity as a downloaded movie from Netflix and that endless mad synchronicities would certainly swirl around me. But…

Nothing nothing nothing.

It's not that I sense any 'deadness', as such; it's just that the energies seeming to flow unceasingly from NicNeven have stopped. Not deadness, no, just a steady stream of, well, *ordinariness*. And that is somewhat startling in a gentle sort of way. M says this always happens to me; I suppose she would know.

I would add that it's Tuesday today, the day of Mars, and I'm in the Atrium, and what I assumed/believed was the University of the Third Age has just gone stampeding out through the doors into a very gray morning. I say 'assumed/believed' because I've learned that this is *not* the U3A, which actually meets elsewhere on another day.

There is a large Enquiries desk in the Atrium so I ask the person in charge:

What's the name of the that walking group?
I don't know, sir.
Where do they walk to?
I really don't know. I can't imagine where.

Well, that must mean they are absolutely positively *definitely* a manifestation of the Wild Hunt that ordinary folk can't see - a collection of cheerfully-dead souls with stout walking shoes heading into the centre of a dying town for blissful release. I suppose I'll join them one day.

Still, there's a teaching in that also. There are infinite tales of mysticks, seers, magicians and channellers who mis-identify the energies/entities they make contact with, yet still get worthwhile results. Perhaps a seer from the remote past (which is also the remote future) might link with me 'now' and identify me as someone else from my genetic and historical lineage: my grandfather, perhaps, with a very different personality to mine. If they're doing that 'now' as I sit here in the Atrium I will say:

Don't rationalise, or the contact will break. All is One. Go with the flow. Just visualise me as a cheery chappy, an absolute hunk and a god among men. As long as I'm not seen as a Sunderland supporter.

Hmmm...
When I arrived here I tried to go on the computer to get a few more drips of information about Christsondy but the PCs are all dead, as though the internet and the rolling billows of the astral light are acting in sympathy. Also, on the way in to the Atrium, I notice that nothing has yet been done about the rubbish in the River Biss that I reported to the appropriate Ascended Masters within the upper floors of the Shamballah that is County Hall. So I can't even send a stinging email full of sound and fury demanding instant clear-ups of the Biss.

M tells me that there *has* been a Bank Holiday and that people *are* allowed time off from work, but I find that a very weak argument.

Maybe when the Biss is clear, the contacts will return...

Tonight, apparently, it will be a very rare Blue Super Moon. I hope I'm not too tired to see it. I suppose, logically, we would drive down to the top of the White Horse at Westbury and watch it from there, but I still get tired easily after the cardiac Event. So I'm tempted to set an alarm and go down to our long and narrow garden and watch it sail across.

For some reason though, despite the lack of flow, I woke up this morning to get my own book *Gate of Moon* from our Upper Room. I haven't looked at it in years, and feel no need to re-read the text, but I remembered that there were some line drawings that I did in 1981/2, when I was alone in my flat on Winsley Hill drawing madly, trying to capture energies/entities/beings/parts-of-myself.

I suppose that one of them was, in a sense, of Christsondy! Has he been here all along? Is that the River Biss? And is that a whorl I see before mine eyes? We do have a sort of 'wand' in the garden with the three tines, and a grass snake somewhere under the garden office. And the hierophant of the Ra-Horakhte Temple once 'saw' me with the antlers before I gave a talk on the Horned God and other things in Seattle. As did my dear friend Annie Tod who saw me with the horns before she even knew who I was or what I did, while at the same moment I recognised her as the Lady Tui (long story).

I suppose I should fill my inertia and do a Zen thing and colour it all in.

In the meantime, forgive me for a whole page of flummery...

It's pissing down today after the recent sun but I don't mind. I daresay the Biss is in torrent but I haven't crossed it yet.

I had a restless night last night filled with zombies. I didn't see them as zombies first, and assumed from the bent postures and crooked flailing limbs and horribly wrinkled, drooling faces they were actually from an Old People's home. Their attacks were ruthless and relentless. I screamed once or twice when I found them creeping up behind me but quickly composed myself and fought them off, again and again.

Did I use Banishing Gestures?

No.

Did I Assume a powerful God Form?

Well, yes, but I had imposed upon me the shape and manner of a big cowboy called Mario[17].

I must say, when I got going, I was magnificent.

Of course, this was not the consequences of the inner Work I've been doing with the 15/16th Century Witches of Elphame, but something far healthier. We took 6 of our 8 young grandchildren to the Active Reality gaming place in Bath where one of our missions was to kill as many zombies as possible. My virtual Big Cowboy (and I've been called that often) was top scorer and I probably saved the world. M, bless her, did her best but her handling of the Glock was, frankly, somewhat amateurish.

I had no idea what to expect. It felt astonishing to enter this Virtual World by means of the ultra-high tech goggles. Don't they put masks on candidates for admission to some of the Mysteries – or is that just Freemasonry? - Or that place with the red light down a back-alleyway in Trowbridge that was raided recently?

The kids all wanted to go again. So do we.

As for the Blue Super Moon, I went down to the garden at 2am and watch it for a while next to our faery gate, but it was neither blue nor particularly super in size. I took a photo but it came out rubbish. The zombies proved far more impressive.

_____

17 A name of Italian origin, meaning '*manly*'.

It's Friday today, the day of Venus. We're getting things ready for a week at Mwmbwls (aka Mumbles) from Saturday. Last night I got down two books from the Upper Room to take with me: *The Fairy Faith in Celtic Countries* by Wossisname[18]; and *The Secret Initiation of Jesus at Qumran: The Essene Mysteries of John the Baptist* by Robert Feather. The former should need no introduction, though I haven't read it for decades. The second is about the subtle and perhaps secret influence of Akhnaton upon the Essenes and John the Baptist. That book came to me a few years ago because the Library Service was about to bin it, as no-one ever read it. But I'm now quite startled…

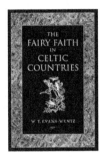

After my usual cuppa at Leykers I donated a couple of books to one of the Charity Shops (that I now think of as Portals) and as I was leaving I saw a small box of gew-gaws amid the bric-a-brac. The woman behind the counter said that some anonymous soul had dropped off a carrier bag containing stuff – little resin statuettes and icons - from Cairo Museum.

They aren't very old and I can't imagine they have any intrinsic value. They were almost certainly bought from the gift shop there a few decades ago. Yet the first one I picked up was of the Lady Tui/Tiye, whom I mentioned apropos of nothing only the other day! The original statuette of Tui depicted a high status woman

18 I've learned, without surprise, that Tolkien used this book as a source of reference.

from the reign of Amenhotep III to Akhenaten (ca. 1390–1349 B.C); Dynasty 18 of the New Kingdom of Ancient Egypt. She is presumed to have been a leading servant of the powerful Great Royal Wife Tiye (her superior, with whom she may have shared the same name), and her title has been variously translated over the years as 'Chief of Weavers'[19] and 'Chief of the Household' and even 'Mistress of the Harem'. The late great Billie-John, who co-authored our *Inner Guide to Egypt*, did an excellent line drawing of Tui for that book. So I bought the Resin Lady for £2.00, along with another small and rather horny piece depicting a full length naked goddess, almost certainly Nu/Nut/Nuit[20], also for £2.00.

(I say 'horny' because for some reason it made me remember the teenage pervy dreams I had about Moina Mathers, and what she might look like if she took all her clothes off for me.)

Somewhat buzzing from all this I paced across town to the library, saying hello to the River Biss (which might have transformed itself into the River Nile) but before I entered the hallowed halls of the Atrium I knew to HAD to return immediately and get two other pieces, one of which was a larger figure of Akhnaton. Well, that was odd too because,

---

19 So here she is now in a town of former Weavers!
20 Yes, Nut, from an engraving on the sarcophagus of Djedhor. I've never seen Her standing straight, before.

as I said, only last night I got Robert Feather's learned book down from our Upper Room to take with me on holiday to Mwmbwls.

So it seems that Akhnaton wasn't going to be left out, and I suppose that was always him all over in his heyday. I was never an admirer. That statuette cost a massive £4.00, but I couldn't quibble could I? Oh and I bought a neat little pyramid. There were several other un-interesting pieces in there including a small Osiris, which is also odd because I got a post today from Judith Page saying she'd dedicated her book *Osiris* to me and Billie-John. In the box were two bits of stone that had obviously been removed from some holy place when the guards and guides weren't looking but I don't want that sort of energy in our house. I still haven't cleaned these artefacts up yet, and don't know where I will put them - probably in a secret nook of our long and narrow garden. [21]

Yes, yes I went back for Osiris. How could I not? It was the Osirian energies ('*...the force that through the green fuse drives the flower*' as Dylan Thomas wrote) that inspired *Earth God Rising* after a strange solo Working at Conkwell on Winsley Hill.

He/It/They was one of the first recorded Green Men and a Horned God in his own rite, although Judith Page always thought of him as the Dickless Wonder and she assures me that her recent book is **not** a eulogy!

I also knew that I now HAD to buy (£1 each) the two pieces of stone that had been filched from some far-off temple from the heart of Khem. Had I not, the shop-keeper might have just seen them as rubbish and dumped them in the bin. I'm not sensitive enough to know what sort of energies they might contain, but I'll have a good talk to them, introduce mySelf to them as Khasekhemwy or even Sekhemket, show them around their new site and give them a good loving home under our garden office, which is a sort of temple. I'll let you know if it all goes horribly wrong.

---

21 I've since found a final piece depicting Hathor, a favourite Neter of mine.

Not a good picture, but here they are on a shelf in the garden office: Akhnaton, Osiris, Lady Tui, Pyramid. That photo behind is of Margaret being fired out of a cannon – honest. I think Akhnaton might need to go into the garden itself, near the faery gate, but I'll negotiate with the Good People there first.

I'm knackered now after all the inner excitement.

Peace peace peace to all of them.

Holy Hiatus here. Scribbling this on holiday in the Gower again. Evans-Wentz describes the 'peculiar' folk-lore conditions that he felt existed in the Gower peninsular 'due to the present population being by ancestry English and Flemish as well as Cornish and Welsh.' He adds that despite this, Brythonic beliefs have generally survived here, especially featuring pixies and the 'Verry Volk' - who love plenty of musick and dancing.

I'll keep an eye out for them. Or would, except I've got a rotten dose of the 'flu and just want to sleep all the time. Am I being enchanted? For a hundred years?

We're near the beach where Dylan Thomas used to cycle to as a boy; not far from where the Red Lady of Paviland was found, also near where the Red *Lad*'s [sic] Continuation as Stan Gooch died in extreme poverty in a caravan site.

Death shall have no dominion, says I.

M. is plodging in the sea at low tide. I'm in the cafe watching her. The beach is is huge and golden and curved like a druid's scythe and almost empty.

I'm still struck by the unexpected 'flow' of recent magickal currents. Last week (or was it last month?) I scribbled a brief sentence apropos of nothing about the Lady Tui from the Old Land of Ancient Egypt. When I came to type it up and posh out the prose I wondered if this was, in the context of Elphame, totally irrelevant. *I'll tidy that up tomorrow*, I thought. Yet 24 hours later I stumbled on those old icons from Cairo Museum (or so they told me), on a lower shelf in a nondescript Charity Shop in the oft-scorned and decaying centre of Trowbridge.

It must be the Bo-ah thing again. 'I' might be operating along that straight line from past to future whose spirals brush me lightly. And it seems that whenever I try hard to get results I rarely get an immediate response. Yet I must have created undercurrents that enable things to pop up like bollards.

Although it's Tuesday and we're back from holiday and I'm in the Atrium there's no sign of the Wild Hunt. Maybe they only ever existed in a different realm after all? The blistering heat of last week has gone but on the way in I noticed that the grocery cart and bollards have still not been removed from the River Biss. I'd do it myself if I could reach and if I was fit. So another stinging letter to the Council will be on its way soon.

Have finally got a date for the removal of the Mab Stone at the hospital in Bath on Thursday. I can't say I'm not scared. The procedure itself is straightforward if unpleasant; it's the possibility of a repeat of the complications that arose afterwards that frightens me. With a weakened heart since then, I fear the obvious and am wondering if this present Journal might be my Last Hurrah. I must try to get it all into shape and forge a conclusion of sorts, if that's what I'm meant to do.

Really, it has been a simply strange and strangely simple flow of magick in my life from the very first appearance of the Astral News-sheet proclaiming the word Elphame. When I started really hoped that I would be granted Tolkien-like glimpses of that realm akin to those described by seers like Yeats, AE, Kim Seymour, Wendy Berg, Bob Stewart and all the other visionaries I've always envied. Yet what I've experienced has been what I can only call a 'flow', a to and fro of energies, rippling with events, incidents, imaginal but very real people, thoughts, ideas and surprises and synchonicities that have shown this derelict little and apparently inconsequential town of Trowbridge and its puny little River Biss to be a Continuation of Elphame in its own rite and right.

Hmmmm...

I was pretty much minding my own business and feeling somewhat glum when a slim young fella sat opposite me on the small table in the very centre of the Atrium from where the Wild Hunt would normally manifest then surge away.

125

Nice hat, Walter[22] I said, recognising him at once, cleverly acknowledging the years he spent with 'Red Hat' monks in Tibet, and added: *I'm largely finished reading your first book.*

I pushed said book across to him.

Oh gee, 'The Fairy Faith in Celtic Lands'! It's still going strong. No-one seems interested in the ones I did on Tibetan Buddhism.

He seemed sad. I'm the same when my life-blood books are forgotten or – more usually – completely unknown.

Walter, that Tibetan Buddhism was just a flash in the pan. Today's world wants faeries red in tooth and claw, hot and horny, wild and wonderful. There's even a 'Fairy Shop' in Mumbles entirely devoted to them. Listen, son, I'm going to pick a paragraph from this True Classic of yours at random to see if you can resolve my present stasis re faeries.

So I closed my eyes, riffled the pages like a tarot deck and jabbed my finger like wand onto page 107. He smiled and leaned over, curious at what I had divined. I read it out to him, softly:

> It was nearing sunset now, and a long mountain-climb was ahead of us, and one more visit that evening. When we reached the mountain-side, one of the rarest of Barra's sights greeted us. To the north and south in the golden glow of a September twilight we saw the long line of the Outer Hebrides like the rocky backbone of some submerged continent. The scene and colours on the land and ocean and in the sky seemed more like some magic vision, reflected from Faerie by the 'good people' for our delight, than a thing of our own world. Never was air clearer or sea calmer, nor could there be air sweeter than that in the mystic mountain-stillness holding the perfume of millions of tiny blossoms of purple and white heather; and as the last honey-bees

---

22   Walter Evans-Wentz, 1878-1965, from Trenton, New Jersey.

were leaving the beautiful blossoms their humming came to our
ears like low, strange music from Fairyland...

He sighed, and I think I fell in love with him. The fact is, the more I read about his adventures in 1907 across Ireland, Wales, the Inner and Outer Hebrides, Highland Scotland, the Isle of Man, Cornwall and Brittany the more I envied him. If I could have pre-incarnated as anyone else I suppose I would have chosen him, although I suspect he was probably a 'confirmed bachelor' and that wouldn't have appealed to me at all. Walter was determined to track down and record the last memories of the Fairy Faith and did so by interviewing and living with what one critic described as 'peasants'. That was used in the pejorative sense. I hope that that critic's balls off for being such a snob. I like to think of the term 'peasant' as the French think of the 'paysan' – a person who makes a living from the natural resources of the world, innately noble, attached to the Land and its Mysteries, and not a socio-economic failure grubbing around in downmarket and decaying places.

Walter Walter Walter... many people, no matter how long they live, never get to experience that single moment of Earth Bliss. Perhaps, in these final years of mine, I've been flowing into all along: little whorls and ripples here and there.

*Then perhaps **you're** a Continuation of me, Alan!*

One of many, Walter. I'd be honoured to think so. But you never did come to any conclusion about the 'true' nature of Faeries, did you? I don't think I will even attempt to do so. I'm happy just to flow along.

Don't you really want to find NicNeven?

Well, yes, but maybe even NicNeven is a Continuation of, say, Nuit, or the Lady Tui, and I've been experiencing her via these cosmic-but-personal Originals? Perhaps everyone has got there own cosmic-but-personal Original for NicNeven just rippling away inside. What do you think?

I turned my head for a moment to wave and nod to a former boss of mine from the Library Service who had come clattering toward me with loud threats of speed. But when I looked back Walter had gone, presumably to one of the Bardos that he was one of the first Westerners to explore.

127

I think I'll stop here and tidy the manuscript. I've got the removal of the Mab Stone tomorrow. Although the procedure will straightforward and unpleasant (like 5 years ago), the complications I had afterward almost killed me. Now, with a weakened heart, I'm somewhat anxious. I suppose I should tail off with an inspiring paragraph about how everyone, no matter where they live and in what benighted circumstances, can soon find 'Continuations' of faerie in their own lives and create their own sense of Elphame.

So, just in case the Fae are about to summon me home, I will secretly leave full instructions printed out on my pc in the garden office so that M can publish this via KDP after my death – for whatever it might be worth. There's still so much I don't understand and probably never will.

Sorry to sound miserable…

Printed in Great Britain
by Amazon

28256911R00076